(18)

SPMG

N

CW01649220

5

New Heinemann Maths

# Textbook

Heinemann

Heinemann Educational Publishers
Halley Court, Jordan Hill, Oxford OX2 8EJ
a division of Reed Educational and Professional Publishing Ltd

Heinemann is a registered trademark of Reed Educational and Professional Publishing Ltd



**Writing team**
John T Blair
Percy W Farren
Myra A Pearson
Dorothy S Simpson
John W Thayers
David K Thomson



First Published 2001

06 05 04 03 02 01
10 9 8 7 6 5 4 3 2 1

ISBN 0 435 17646 3

Typeset and layout by Mandy Emery.
Illustrated by Debbie Clark, David Till, David Kearney, Jon Mitchell, Derek Brazell, Diane Fawcett and Tony O'Donnell.
Cover Illustation by Mark Oliver.
Printed and bound by Edelvives, Zaragoza.

# Contents

| | TEXTBOOK | EXTENSION TEXTBOOK |
|---|---|---|
| **Division** | | |
| By 2-10 | 47–48 | |
| By 10, 100, 1000 | 49 | |
| Divisibility by 4, 10, 5, 2, 100 | 50 | |
| Link with multiplication | 51 | |
| Using and applying, linking multiplication and division | 52 | |
| Three-digit numbers by 2-9 | 53 | |
| Remainders | 54 | |
| Using and applying, rounding | 55 | |
| | | E6–7 |
| **Fractions** | | |
| Sevenths, ninths, twelfths and twentieths | 56 | |
| Equivalence | 57 | |
| Comparing and ordering | 58 | |
| Of a set, numerator 1/ numerator > 1 | 59–60 | |
| Hundredths of a set/quantity | 61 | |
| **Decimals** | | |
| Tenths, notation/sequences/ comparing and ordering/rounding | 62–63 | |
| Tenths, mental addition, subtraction | 64–66 | |
| Tenths, written addition, subtraction | 67–68 | |
| Tenths, multiplication | 69 | E8 |
| Hundredths, notation/sequences/ place value, comparing and ordering | 70–71 | |
| Hundredths, mental addition/subtraction | 72 | |
| Hundredths, written addition/subtraction | 73 | |
| Using and applying, calculator | 74 | E9 |
| **Percentages** | | |
| Concept | 75 | |
| Relationships, one whole is 100% | 76 | E10 |
| **Number properties** | | |
| Negative numbers | 77–78 | |
| Sequences | 79 | |
| Multiples, factors | 80–81 | |
| | | E11–12 |
| **Area** | | |
| Formula for a rectangle, $cm^2$ | 82 | |
| Irregular shapes by formula | 83 | |
| Square metres, $m^2$ | 84 | |
| | | E14–15 |
| **Time** | | |
| 24-hour times, using and applying | 85–86 | |
| 24-hour times past/to the hour, durations | 87 | |
| Using and applying, timetables | 88 | |

**1** **(a)** Jamie has 2170 stamps.
He buys 10 more.
How many stamps has Jamie now?

**(b)** Polly has 1880 stamps.
She buys 100 more.
How many stamps has Polly now?

**2**

**(a)** 10 more than 6000

**(b)** 10 more than 5496

**(c)** 10 less than 2562

**(d)** 10 less than 3400

**(e)** 100 more than 9900

**(f)** 100 more than 4732

**(g)** 100 less than 6123

**(h)** 100 less than 10 000

**(i)** 50 more than 9700

**(j)** 50 more than 1950

**(k)** 50 less than 4000

**(l)** 50 less than 8300

**3** **Alan** **Benjy** **Cara** **Daljit** **Emma** **Faye**

How many stamps does each person have after

**(a)** Alan gives Benjy 100 stamps **(b)** Cara gives Emma 50 stamps

**(c)** Faye gives Daljit 10 stamps?

**4** Write the multiples of 10 between

**(a)** 3210 and 3250 **(b)** 6480 and 6520 **(c)** 8015 and 7975

**5** Write **a** multiple of 100 between

**(a)** 2500 and 2100 **(b)** 7806 and 8206 **(c)** 10 000 and 9600

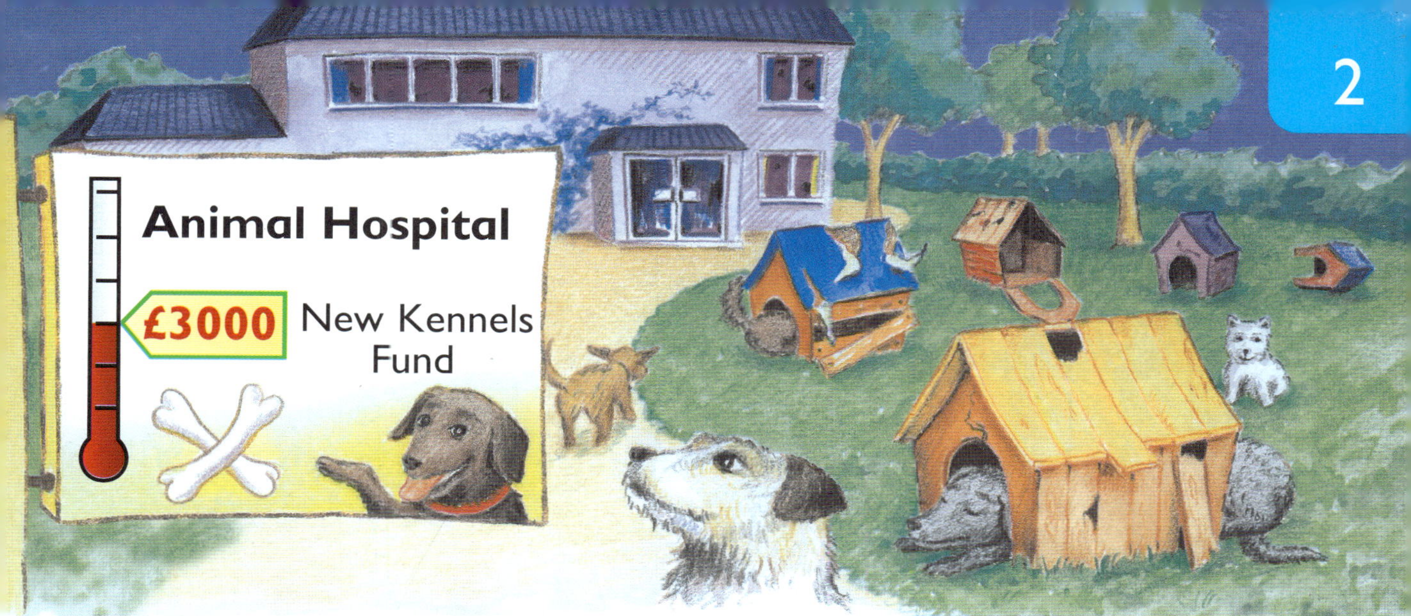


**1** How much money is in the New Kennels Fund after it is given **£1000 more?**

**2** Write each amount.

**(a)** £1000 more
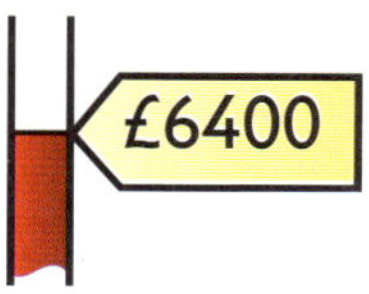


**(b)** £1000 more
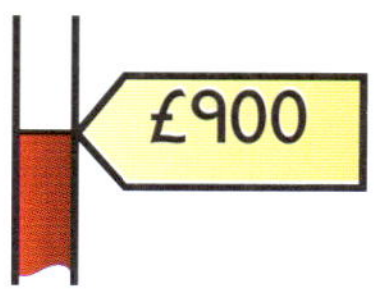


**(c)** £1000 less
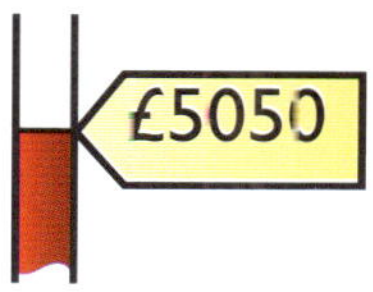


**(d)** £1000 less
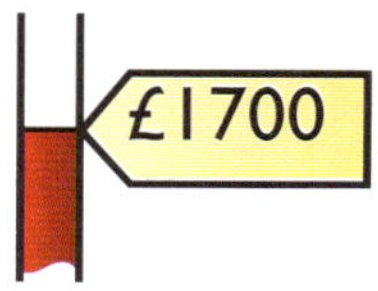


**(e)** £500 more
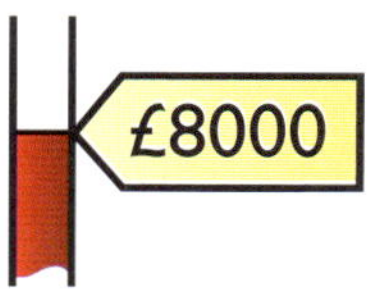


**(f)** £500 less
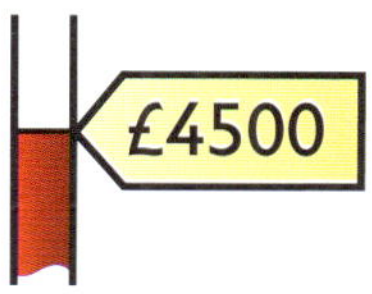


**(g)** £500 more
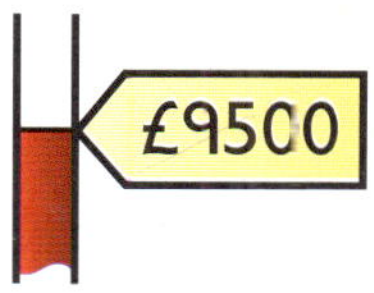


**(h)** £500 less
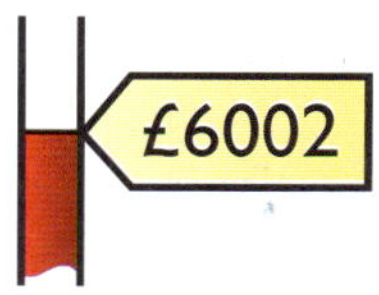


**(i)** £1000 more
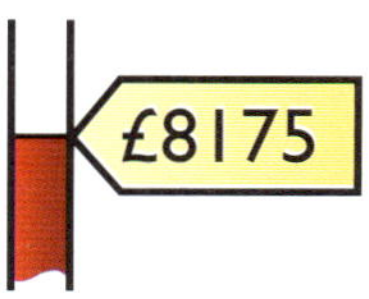


**(j)** £1000 less
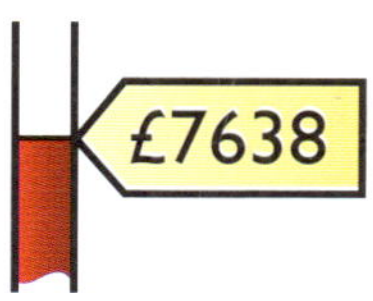


**(k)** £1000 more
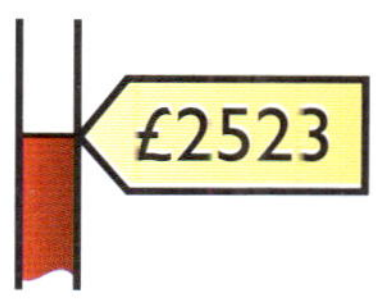


**(l)** £1000 less
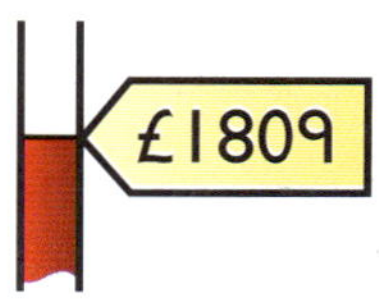


**3** Write the multiple of 1000
**(a)** after 2000 **(b)** before 8731.

**4** Which muliple of 1000 is between
**(a)** 4000 and 6000 **(b)** 7294 and 6294?

**1** **10 000 more** people attended the Thistle v **United** match.
What was the size of this crowd?

**2** Write the number 10 000 more than
**(a)** 60 000 **(b)** 37 489 **(c)** 90 000 **(d)** 141 000

**3** Write the number 10 000 less than
**(a)** 70 000 **(b)** 58 673 **(c)** 15 000 **(d)** 200 000

**4**

**Weekly Sport**

Thistle v Rovers—
Ticket Sales total £120 000

Ticket sales for the Thistle v **United** match totalled **£100 000 more**.
How much did this crowd pay for tickets?

**5** Write the amount £100 000 more than
**(a)** £700 000 **(b)** £350 000 **(c)** £900 000 **(d)** £404 000

**6** Write the amount £100 000 less than
**(a)** £600 000 **(b)** £870 000 **(c)** 1 000 000 **(d)** £111 111

**7** *SporTV* paid £3 000 000 to film matches last season and **£1 000 000 more** this season.
How much did *SporTV* pay to film matches this season?

**8** Find £1 000 000 more than
**(a)** £5 000 000 **(b)** £17 000 000
**(c)** £8 500 000 **(d)** £9 006 006

**9** Find £1 000 000 less than
**(a)** £4 000 000 **(b)** £16 000 000
**(c)** £10 200 000 **(d)** £4 400 044

**1** What is the value of the **2** in each number?

(a) 63 428
(b) 456 213
(c) 9 431 892
(d) 15 428 079
(e) 10 200 000
(f) 662 374

**2** What is the value of the red digit in each number?

(a) 289 **4**61
(b) 7 50**2** 150
(c) 12 0**3**8 420
(d) **1** 347 916

**3**

| | | |
|---|---|---|
| 2 430 493 | 7 340 700 | 10 150 520 |
| 2 340 630 | 3 150 303 | 1 180 102 |

Which number
(a) has 340 thousands and an even hundreds digit
(b) is greater than 6 million and has tens digit 0
(c) has 150 thousands and 3 units
(d) has 2 millions and fewer than 5 hundreds?

**4** Use the digits 3 4 6 7 9 to make a number which

(a) is greater than fifty thousand
(b) has a tens digit double the units digit
(c) has a hundreds digit equal to the sum of the units and tens digits.

| | Number made | Number still to be made |
|---|---|---|
| **1** **(a)** | 84 325 | 100 |
| **(b)** | 193 400 | 100 000 |
| **(c)** | 250 705 | 1000 |
| **(d)** | 1 480 000 | 10 000 |

How many of each item will be made altogether?

**2** How many of each item are **not** faulty?

**(a)** 192 420 → 1000 are faulty.

**(b)** 530 650 → 10 000 are faulty.

**(c)** 1 170 000 → 100 000 are faulty.

**3** Increase 1 358 247 by

**(a)** one thousand **(b)** one hundred **(c)** ten thousand
**(d)** ten **(e)** one million **(f)** one hundred thousand.

**4** Decrease 5 346 295 by

**(a)** one million **(b)** ten **(c)** one hundred thousand
**(d)** ten thousand **(e)** one hundred **(f)** one thousand.

**5** **(a)** 269 450 + 1000 **(b)** 1 792 800 + 100 000
**(c)** 3 604 240 − 10 000 **(d)** 10 230 020 − 1 000 000

**1**

Enter these numbers in your calculator.
Record each display **using numerals**.

**(a)** Fourteen thousand six hundred and twenty.

**(b)** One hundred and twenty-five thousand, eight hundred and nine.

**(c)** Three million, seven hundred and two thousand, four hundred.

**(d)** Ten million, three hundred and seventy thousand, eight hundred and eighty.

**2** Start with [1 542 360] each time. Add

**(a)** 100 **(b)** 1000 **(c)** 10 000 **(d)** 1 000 000

**3** Start with [12 673 458] each time. Subtract

**(a)** 1000 **(b)** 10 **(c)** 100 000 **(d)** 10 000 000

**Check each answer with a calculator.**

**4** What has been **added** to change each display?

**(a)** [43 200] → [43 300] **(b)** [614 070] → [615 070]

**(c)** [135 060] → [235 060] **(d)** [5 801 250] → [6 801 250]

What has been **subtracted** to change each display?

**(e)** [94 150] → [94 140] **(f)** [205 739] → [204 739]

**(g)** [4 240 000] → [3 240 000] **(h)** [568 127] → [558 127]

1 Write the larger number.

(a) 306 545    306 554     (b) 7 425 800    7 415 900

2 Write the smaller number.

(a) 6 990 350    6 810 710     (b) 10 499 999    10 599 100

3 Which number is **(a)** largest **(b)** smallest?

| | | |
|---|---|---|
| 2 640 600 | 930 334 | 2 630 700 |
| 930 434 | 2 640 700 | 930 443 |

4 List in order.

**(a)** Start with the largest.

143 850    314 580    548 310    341 085    538 140

**(b)** Start with the smallest.

649 200    3 600 310    648 350    640 990    3 600 250

5 Write True (T) **or** False (F).

**(a)** 74 500 < 75 400     **(b)** 1 650 000 > 1 560 000

6 Complete using > or <.

**(a)** 135 000 ■ 235 000     **(b)** 3 198 000 ■ 3 189 000

**(c)** 787 780 ■ 787 807     **(d)** 10 342 600 ■ 10 346 200

**1** Write the clipboard numbers so that they are **all** correct.

| | |
|---|---|
| Fifty-four thousand, three hundred and twenty. | 54 302 |
| One hundred and thirteen thousand and twenty-seven. | 113 207 |
| Six million, five hundred thousand. | 6 050 000 |
| Two million, sixty thousand and eight. | 2 060 008 |

**2** Write each number using **numerals**.

**(a)** Forty-eight thousand, seven hundred and ninety.

**(b)** One hundred and thirty thousand.

**(c)** Fifteen thousand, six hundred and five.

**(d)** One hundred and eighty-five thousand, four hundred.

**(e)** Thirty thousand, two hundred and fourteen.

**(f)** Seven million, two hundred thousand, one hundred and six.

**3** Write **in words**.

**(a)** 24 000 **(b)** 640 000 **(c)** 73 800
**(d)** 102 650 **(e)** 3 400 000 **(f)** 10 002 036

**1** Medals were given to the first hundred runners to complete a Fun Run.

What colour is the medal for

**(a)** thirty-fourth  **(b)** fifty-seventh  **(c)** sixty-second
**(d)** eighty-first  **(e)** ninety-sixth  **(f)** seventy-fifth?

**2** Write each person's position.

I was twenty-ninth.

**Gindy**

I finished in fortieth place.

**Sue**

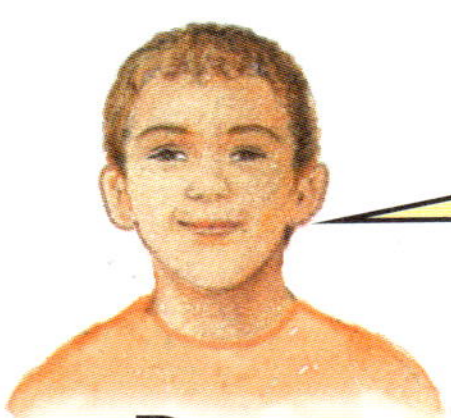

I finished seventy-third.

**Dave**

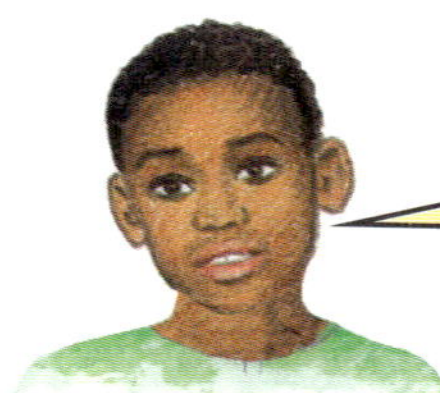

I was fifty-eighth.

**Ben**

I was three places behind Sue.

**Li**

I was five places ahead of Dave.

**Jean**

**3** Write in words.

**(a)** 35th  **(b)** 27th  **(c)** 52nd  **(d)** 99th

**1** Estimate. About how many kilometres

- has each tanker travelled

- has each yacht travelled

- has each fishing boat travelled?

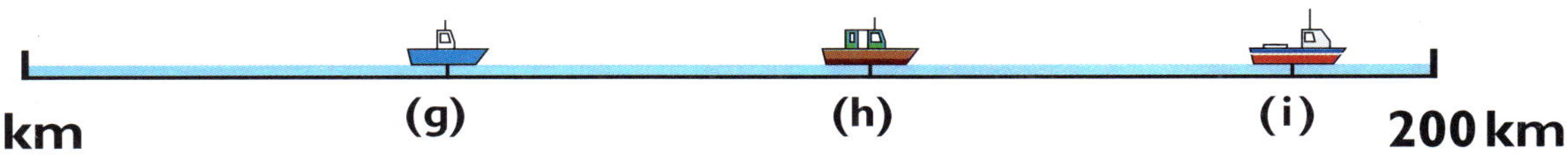


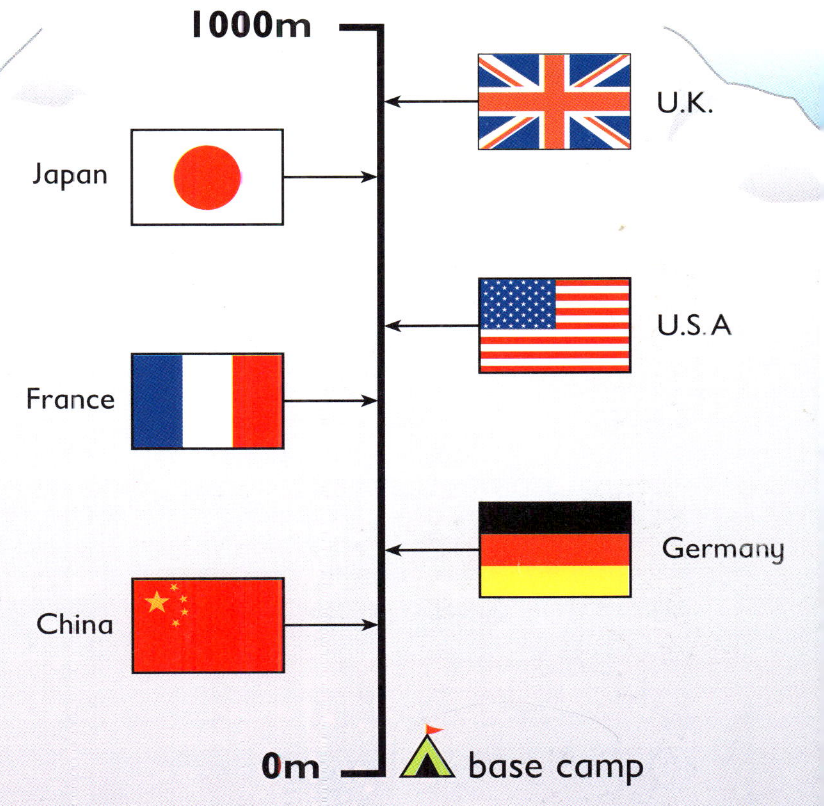


**2** Estimate the height, in metres, climbed from the base camp by each country's mountaineers.

**1** Write each price to the **nearest hundred** pounds.

**(a)** Computer

£845

**(b)** CD system

£405

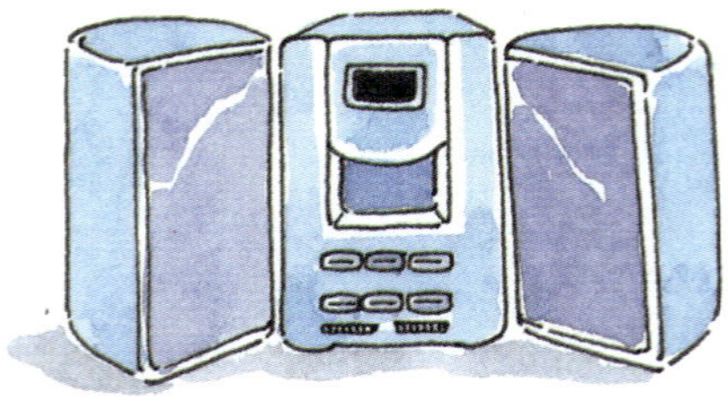

**(c)** Camcorder

£777

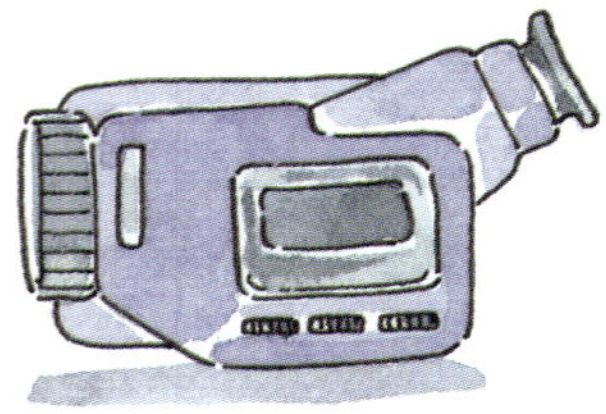

**(d)** £91 **(e)** £450 **(f)** £969

**2** Write each price to the **nearest ten** pounds.

**(a)** DVD player

£212

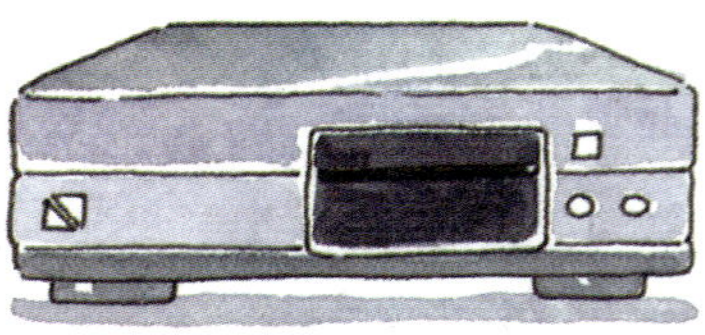

**(b)** Television

£994

**(c)** Microwave

£146

**(d)** £303 **(e)** £628 **(f)** £195

**3** Write the price of each of these items

- to the nearest hundred pounds **and**
- to the nearest ten pounds.

**(a)** Mountain bike £249
**(b)** Washing machine £557
**(c)** Antique vase £185
**(d)** Digital camera £223
**(e)** Gold watch £651
**(f)** Football season ticket £318
**(g)** Aeroplane ticket to Australia £472
**(h)** Designer clothes outfit £399

**1** List the numbers

**(a)** nearer to 8000 than 7000

**(b)** nearer to 6400 than 6300

**(c)** nearer to 3770 than 3760.

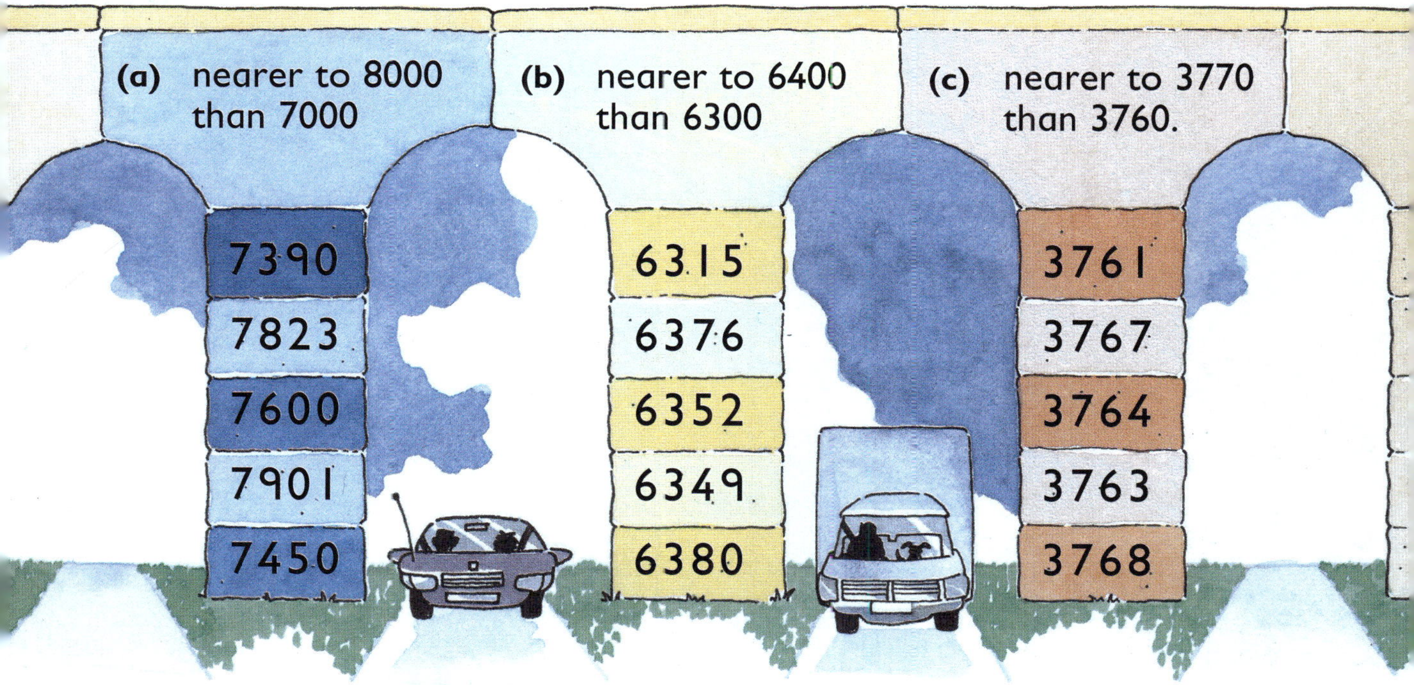


**2** Write

- to the nearest thousand

**(a)** 5055 **(b)** 3333 **(c)** 736 **(d)** 9500

- to the nearest hundred

**(e)** 4281 **(f)** 8050 **(g)** 2111 **(h)** 1042

- to the nearest ten

**(i)** 9012 **(j)** 4784 **(k)** 3625 **(l)** 3996

**3** Write the number of miles each car has travelled

**(a)** to the nearest thousand

**(b)** to the nearest hundred

**(c)** to the nearest ten.

**1** Double each number.

(a) 61 (b) 74 (c) 83 (d) 54 (e) 92

(f) 94 (g) 53 (h) 72 (i) 81

**2** Write each number on a **red** ticket with its double on a **yellow** ticket.

Red tickets: 58, 77, 86, 99, 65, 56

Yellow tickets: 112, 130, 198, 172, 154, 116

**3**

(a) Double 57 (b) Double 89 (c) Double 66

(d) 96 + 96 (e) 67 + 67 (f) 59 + 59

**4**

(a) 63 + 64 (b) 83 + 82 (c) 55 + 56 (d) 71 + 72

(e) 88 + 87 (f) 98 + 99 (g) 76 + 75 (h) 68 + 69

(i) 63 + 65 (j) 75 + 77 (k) 87 + 89 (l) 96 + 98

**1** Write each number on a box with its double on a label.

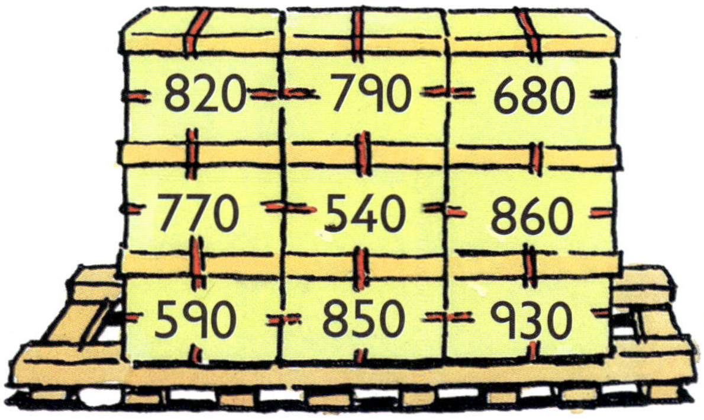


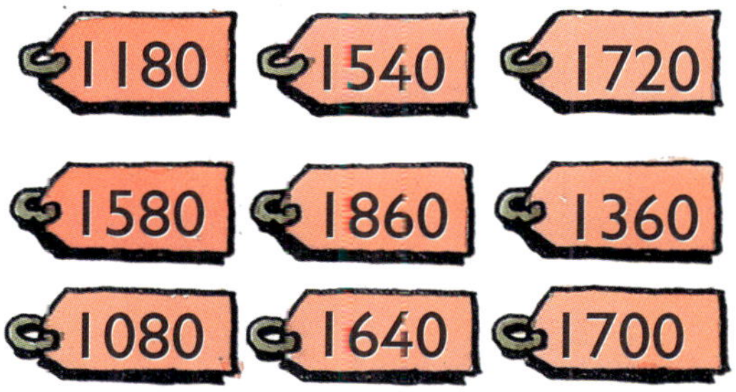


**2** Double each number.

(a) 740 (b) 5600 (c) 4900

(d) 8800 (e) 990 (f) 9500

(g) 1700 (h) 5700 (i) 2600

**3**

**4** Which number when doubled gives

(a) 1020 (b) 1600 (c) 14 200 (d) 15 000?

1 What is the total weight of each set of packages.

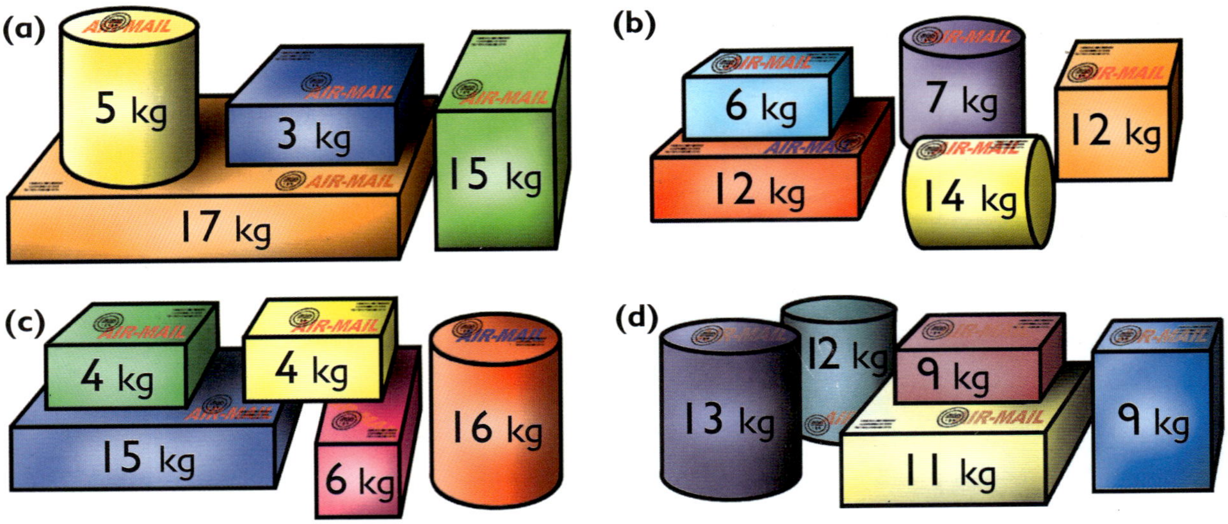


2 (a) 6 + 12 + 14 + 9 + 4 (b) 16 + 7 + 8 + 13 + 6
(c) 5 + 9 + 11 + 9 + 15 (d) 17 + 4 + 9 + 17 + 16

3 Find the total volume in each set of tanks.

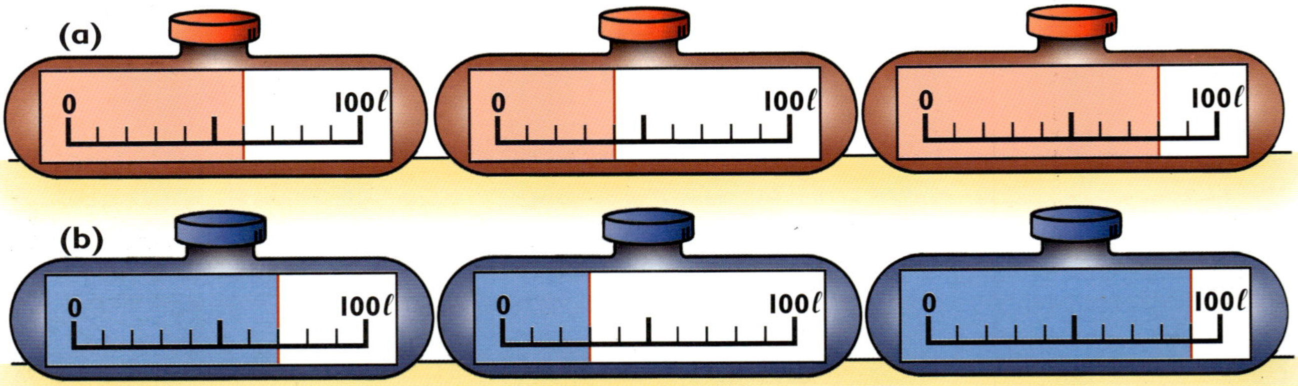


4 (a) 40 + 70 + 80 (b) 70 + 60 + 40 (c) 50 + 30 + 70 (d) 90 + 40 + 20

5 Find the total number of passengers carried by each airport taxi.

| Driver | Fri | Sat | Sun |
|---|---|---|---|
| Tom | 24 | 32 | 16 |
| Ahmed | 33 | 27 | 17 |
| Gail | 27 | 36 | 13 |

| Driver | Fri | Sat | Sun |
|---|---|---|---|
| Debbie | 34 | 26 | 14 |
| Pete | 21 | 29 | 19 |
| Scott | 15 | 33 | 26 |

# Fruit 'n' Juice

**1 Fruit drinks sold on Saturday.**

Find the total number sold of:

(a)  and 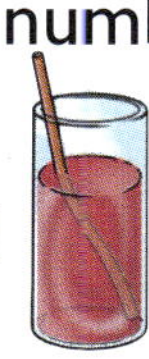

(b)  and 

(c)  and 

(d)  and 

(e)  and 

(f)  and 

**2** (a) 347 + ■ = 417 (b) ■ + 60 = 235 (c) 474 + ■ = 504

**3 Fruit sold in July.**

| | | | |
|---|---|---|---|
| 278 apples | 31 melons | 374 oranges | 49 pineapples |
| 194 bananas | 59 limes | 293 lemons | 41 pears |

Find the total number sold of:

(a) apples and pineapples (b) oranges and limes
(c) pears and bananas (d) lemons and melons
(e) apples and pears (f) pineapples and bananas.

**4** (a) 284 + 29 (b) 363 + 61 (c) 192 + 21
(d) 358 + 59 (e) 177 + 41 (f) 485 + 39
(g) 156 + 72 (h) 434 + 88 (i) 276 + 52

**5** (a) 185 + ■ = 216 (b) 267 + ■ = 316 (c) 533 + ■ = 614
(d) ■ + 39 = 223 (e) ■ + 21 = 217 (f) ■ + 69 = 547

**1** Paulo's Pizza Parlour opened last month.
In the first week Paulo's takings were:

| Mon | Tue | Wed | Thu | Fri | Sat | Sun |
|---|---|---|---|---|---|---|
| £241 | £351 | £400 | £562 | £723 | £832 | £613 |

In the second week Paulo's takings **increased** by:

| Mon | Tue | Wed | Thu | Fri | Sat | Sun |
|---|---|---|---|---|---|---|
| £33 | £44 | £73 | £15 | £36 | £25 | £26 |

What were Paulo's takings for each day in Week 2?

**2** Use your **answers** from question 1.
In the third week Paulo's takings increased by:

| Mon | Tue | Wed | Thu | Fri | Sat | Sun |
|---|---|---|---|---|---|---|
| £74 | £24 | £56 | £17 | £23 | £34 | £27 |

What were Paulo's takings for each day in Week 3?

**3** **(a)** 134 + 77 **(b)** 668 + 64 **(c)** 895 + 46 **(d)** 286 + 57
**(e)** 787 + 65 **(f)** 856 + 86 **(g)** 689 + 34 **(h)** 477 + 36

**4** **(a)** 345 + ■ = 400 **(b)** 431 + ■ = 500 **(c)** 522 + ■ = 600
**(d)** 727 + ■ = 800 **(e)** 964 + ■ = 1000 **(f)** 653 + ■ = 700

**5** **(a)** 226 + ■ = 289 **(b)** 153 + ■ = 198 **(c)** 481 + ■ = 525
**(d)** 765 + ■ = 850 **(e)** 874 + ■ = 927 **(f)** 342 + ■ = 435
**(g)** 147 + ■ = 233 **(h)** 568 + ■ = 655 **(i)** 526 + ■ = 602

**1** How many items are on each of these orders?

(a)

| Ice-Cream Bar Order | |
|---|---|
| **Cones** | |
| chocolate | 120 |
| plain | 140 |

(b)

| Ice-Cream Bar Order | |
|---|---|
| **Wafers** | |
| nougat | 230 |
| plain | 160 |

(c)

| Ice-Cream Bar Order | |
|---|---|
| **Tubs** | |
| small | 370 |
| large | 110 |

(d)

| Ice-Cream Bar Order | |
|---|---|
| **Spoons** | |
| plastic | 410 |
| wooden | 260 |

(e)

| Ice-Cream Bar Order | |
|---|---|
| **Napkins** | |
| white | 220 |
| green | 350 |

(f)

| Ice-Cream Bar Order | |
|---|---|
| **Dishes** | |
| paper | 190 |
| plastic | 310 |

**2**
(a) 360 + 350 = ■ (b) 470 + 340 = ■ (c) 160 + 180 = ■
(d) 240 + 170 = ■ (e) 730 + 180 = ■ (f) 420 + 290 = ■
(g) 230 + ■ = 420 (h) 570 + ■ = 730 (i) ■ + 360 = 620

**3** Find the total number of ice-creams sold.

(a) chocolate (b) raspberry
(c) lemon (d) orange

**4** How many of these were sold?

(a) raspberry and orange **cones**
(b) lemon and chocolate **tubs**

**5** What was the total number sold of

(a) cones (b) tubs?

**6**
(a) 230 + 270 + 220 = ■
(b) 160 + 250 + 340 = ■

**1** What was the total number of each item sold?

**(a)** Cauliflower Combo **(b)** Bean Risotto **(c)** Vegetable Lasagne
**(d)** Stuffed Peppers **(e)** Winter Salad **(f)** Vege-Stew

**2** **(a)** 316 + 280 **(b)** 150 + 136 **(c)** 170 + 211
**(d)** 465 + 120 **(e)** 530 + 128 **(f)** 359 + 340

**3** **(a)** 123 + ■ = 293 **(b)** 110 + ■ = 344 **(c)** 138 + ■ = 588
**(d)** ■ + 240 = 571 **(e)** ■ + 326 = 456 **(f)** ■ + 420 = 562

**4** How many cartons of these soups were sold?

**(a)** Parsnip and Carrot
**(b)** Tomato and Pumpkin
**(c)** Onion and Leek
**(d)** Carrot and Potato
**(e)** Leek and Bean
**(f)** Pumpkin and Onion
**(g)** Bean and Carrot
**(h)** Potato and Parsnip

**5** **(a)** 146 + ■ = 487 **(b)** 453 + ■ = 688 **(c)** 321 + ■ = 483
**(d)** ■ + 215 = 598 **(e)** ■ + 134 = 469 **(f)** ■ + 292 = 599

| Week 1 | Rent | Heating | Cleaning | Stock | Wages |
|---|---|---|---|---|---|
| *Paulo's Pizza Parlour* | £126 | £245 | £138 | £347 | £534 |
| *Ice-Cream Bar* | £104 | £239 | £152 | £356 | £427 |
| *The Vegetable Bowl* | £169 | £213 | £136 | £438 | £465 |

1 In Week 1 how much was spent

(a) by *Paulo's Pizza Parlour* on Heating and Cleaning
(b) by the *Ice-Cream Bar* on Wages and Stock
(c) by *The Vegetable Bowl* on Heating and Rent?

| Week 2 | Rent | Heating | Cleaning | Stock | Wages |
|---|---|---|---|---|---|
| *Paulo's Pizza Parlour* | £137 | £228 | £115 | £329 | £439 |
| *Ice-Cream Bar* | £178 | £254 | £119 | £418 | £516 |
| *The Vegetable Bowl* | £123 | £247 | £145 | £427 | £406 |

2 During Week 1 **and** Week 2 how much altogether did each snack bar pay for

(a) Rent (b) Heating (c) Cleaning (d) Stock (e) Wages?

3 In **Week 2** which snack bar spent

(a) £694 on Rent and Wages
(b) £557 on Heating and Stock
(c) £551 on Cleaning and Wages?

**1** Add the bonus points to find each child's total score.

**2** **(a)** 2568 + 20 **(b)** 70 + 5024 **(c)** 8018 + 90
**(d)** 9402 + 80 **(e)** 5555 + 30 **(f)** 60 + 2033
**(g)** 10 151 + 40 **(h)** 11 362 + 20 **(i)** 10 013 + 70

**3** How many **bonus** points did each child score?

**4** **(a)** 7246 + ■ = 7296 **(b)** 3054 + ■ = 3084 **(c)** 6161 + ■ = 6191

**5** Josh scored 5315 points. Suzi scored 50 points more than Josh.
What was Suzi's score?

**6** Mel scored 10 527 points.
When she added her bonus points her total was 10 587 points.
How many bonus points did she score?

**1** Find each child's score.

**Mark** 597 points plus 

**Kim** 894 points plus 

**Aisha** 747 points plus 

**Annie** 858 points plus 

**Max** 663 points plus 

**Darren** 809 points plus 

**2** **(a)** 759 + 800 **(b)** 336 + 900 **(c)** 500 + 676

**(d)** 634 + 400 **(e)** 300 + 844 **(f)** 927 + 200

**(g)** 500 + 554 **(h)** 417 + 700 **(i)** 874 + 300

**3** How many points are on each child's card?

**4** **(a)** 676 + ■ = 1276 **(b)** 393 + ■ = 1293 **(c)** ■ + 972 = 1872

**(d)** 700 + ■ = 1204 **(e)** 400 + ■ = 1387 **(f)** ■ + 300 = 1107

**5** Todd had a total of 9786 points.
Mai scored 400 points more than Todd.

What was Mai's total score?

| CINEMA AUDIENCE FIGURES | *Multiplex* | *Film Centre* | *Picture Palace* | *Moviemall* | *Cityscreen* |
|---|---|---|---|---|---|
| **Weekdays** (Mon – Thu) | 3326 | 2253 | 1407 | 1716 | 3082 |
| **Weekend** (Fri – Sun) | 4485 | 3069 | 2614 | 2454 | 3925 |

**1** How many people altogether went to see films at these cinemas on **Weekdays**?

**(a)** *Multiplex* and *Film Centre*
**(b)** *Picture Palace* and *Cityscreen*
**(c)** *Film Centre* and *Moviemall*
**(d)** *Cityscreen* and *Moviemall*

**2** How many people altogether went to see films at these cinemas over the **Weekend**?

**(a)** *Film Centre* and *Cityscreen*
**(b)** *Moviemall* and *Multiplex*
**(c)** *Picture Palace* and *Film Centre*
**(d)** *Multiplex* and *Picture Palace*

**3** What was the total number of people who saw films at each cinema on Weekdays **and** over the Weekend?

**4** **(a)** 5648 + 2275 **(b)** 3639 + 4296 **(c)** 7493 + 2876
**(d)** 5959 + 1708 **(e)** 2656 + 6889 **(f)** 4513 + 3487

**5** The table shows the number of seats in each of the 5 cinemas at the ***Multiplex***. Each cinema has 3 film shows every day. How many people altogether see films on a day when **all 5 cinemas are full for all 3 shows?**

| *Multiplex* | Number of seats |
|---|---|
| Cinema 1 | 400 |
| Cinema 2 | 350 |
| Cinema 3 | 150 |
| Cinema 4 | 100 |
| Cinema 5 | 75 |

Ask your teacher how to play this game.

# Target score

3286 plus 774 plus ■ equals 6000.

Add 90 to 11983.

Find the total of 1886 and 3948.

Double ■ is 152 000.

4616 + ■ gives 7001.

Find the sum of 2762 1715 and 2080.

Find the total of 123, 4, 56 and 7890.

Add 99, 87, 65, 43 and 21.

Each ■ is the same **digit**. Find ■.

■■4+6■=286

3852 plus what gives 7452?

2380 add 3260 add 4120.

Find three consecutive numbers which total 600.

Add 277 to the sum of 414 and 236.

Each ■ is the same **digit**. Find ■.

■0■5 + ■0 equals ■145

**Score**

|  |  |
|---|---|
| Blue | 1 point |
| Red | 2 points |
| Green | 3 points |
| Orange | 4 points |

# Furniture and Carpet Sale

**1** Find the **Sale price** of each item.

**(a)**

**(b)**

**(c)**

**(d)**

**(e)**

**(f)**

**2** **(a)** £260 – £80 **(b)** £150 – £60 **(c)** £540 – £70
**(d)** £913 – £30 **(e)** £369 – £90 **(f)** £616 – £50
**(g)** £320 – £■ = £260 **(h)** £■ – £20 = £480 **(i)** £845 – £■ = £785

**3**

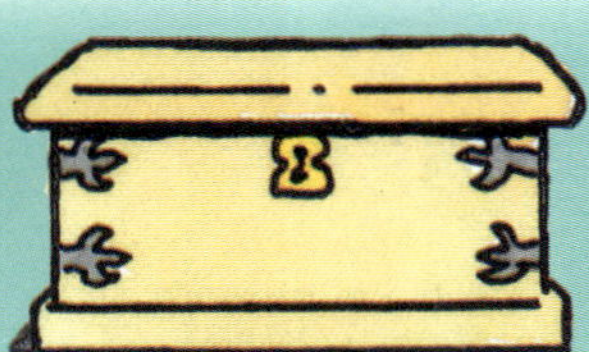
chest £125

stool £71

cabinet £240

lamp £58

Find the difference in price between the

**(a)** cabinet and stool **(b)** lamp and cabinet
**(c)** stool and chest **(d)** chest and lamp.

**4** **(a)** £430 – £49 **(b)** £820 – £92 **(c)** £150 – £81
**(d)** £906 – £88 **(e)** £625 – £41 **(f)** £714 – £39
**(g)** £220 – £■ = £189 **(h)** £400 – £■ = £311 **(i)** £935 – £■ = £884

| CD Title | CDs sold in | |
|---|---|---|
| | January | February |
| a Much More Music | 473 | 34 |
| b Golden Oldies | 154 | 27 |
| c Dance Fever | 260 | 32 |
| d Disco Classics | 67 | 296 |
| e Club Mix | 55 | 391 |
| f Groove Masters | 171 | 47 |
| g Film Themes | 182 | 56 |
| h Rock Dinosaurs | 86 | 194 |
| i Jazz Jive | 16 | 145 |
| j Cool Rap | 352 | 35 |

**1** For each CD, find the difference between the number sold in January and in February.

**2** **(a)** 875 − 27 **(b)** 692 − 24 **(c)** 567 − 18 **(d)** 283 − 65
**(e)** 364 − 45 **(f)** 385 − 77 **(g)** 190 − 43 **(h)** 474 − 58

**3** How many places did each CD rise or fall in the UK Chart between January and February?

## UK CHART PLACINGS

| CD Title | January | February |
|---|---|---|
| a Love Songs | 186 | 37 |
| b Country Breeze | 23 | 141 |
| c Blue Soul | 17 | 132 |
| d Best of TV Soaps | 100 | 84 |
| e Heavy Hits | 76 | 193 |

**1** How many years older is the

(a) Sword than the Helmet
(b) Painting than the Clock
(c) Coin than the Plate
(d) Sword than the Clock
(e) Painting than the Plate
(f) Coin than the Helmet
(g) Coin than the Clock
(h) Sword than the Plate
(i) Painting than the Helmet?

**2**

| | | | |
|---|---|---|---|
| (a) 146 - 65 | (b) 329 - 43 | (c) 617 - 35 | (d) 268 - 87 |
| (e) 704 - 84 | (f) 833 - 73 | (g) 210 - 67 | (h) 730 - 46 |
| (i) 111 - 27 | (j) 351 - 83 | (k) 634 - 67 | (l) 805 - 36 |

**3**

Gold Watch –
made 125 years ago.

Silver Watch –
made 56 years **after** the Gold Watch.

Brass Watch –
made 37 years **after** the Gold Watch.

How many years old is
(a) the Silver Watch
(b) the Brass Watch?

| | Hours of Sunshine | | | | |
|---|---|---|---|---|---|
| | Port Ann | Blue Coast | Long Point | Shell Bay | Cape Fire |
| Spring | 300 | 400 | 190 | 240 | 160 |
| Summer | 710 | 920 | 570 | 480 | 330 |

**1** Find the difference in the hours of sunshine in **Spring** between

**(a)** Port Ann and Long Point
**(b)** Blue Coast and Cape Fire
**(c)** Shell Bay and Port Ann
**(d)** Shell Bay and Blue Coast
**(e)** Long Point and Shell Bay
**(f)** Cape Fire and Shell Bay.

**2** Find the difference in the hours of sunshine in the **Summer** between

**(a)** Long Point and Shell Bay
**(b)** Blue Coast and Long Point
**(c)** Long Point and Port Ann
**(d)** Port Ann and Cape Fire
**(e)** Cape Fire and Long Point
**(f)** Shell Bay and Blue Coast.

**3** In **Autumn**, Port Ann had 610 hours of sunshine.
Find the number of hours of sunshine at

**(a)** Blue Coast → 90 hours less than Port Ann
**(b)** Long Point → 280 hours less than Blue Coast
**(c)** Shell Bay → 150 hours less than Long Point
**(d)** Cape Fire → 670 hours less than Port Ann and Long Point **together.**

**4** **(a)** 700 - ■ = 390
**(b)** 820 - ■ = 550
**(c)** 530 - ■ = 250
**(d)** 940 - ■ = 280
**(e)** ■ - 130 = 470
**(f)** ■ - 290 = 160

**1** The population of **Benvale** is 688.
How many fewer people live in Benvale than in Asham?

**2** Find the difference between these populations:

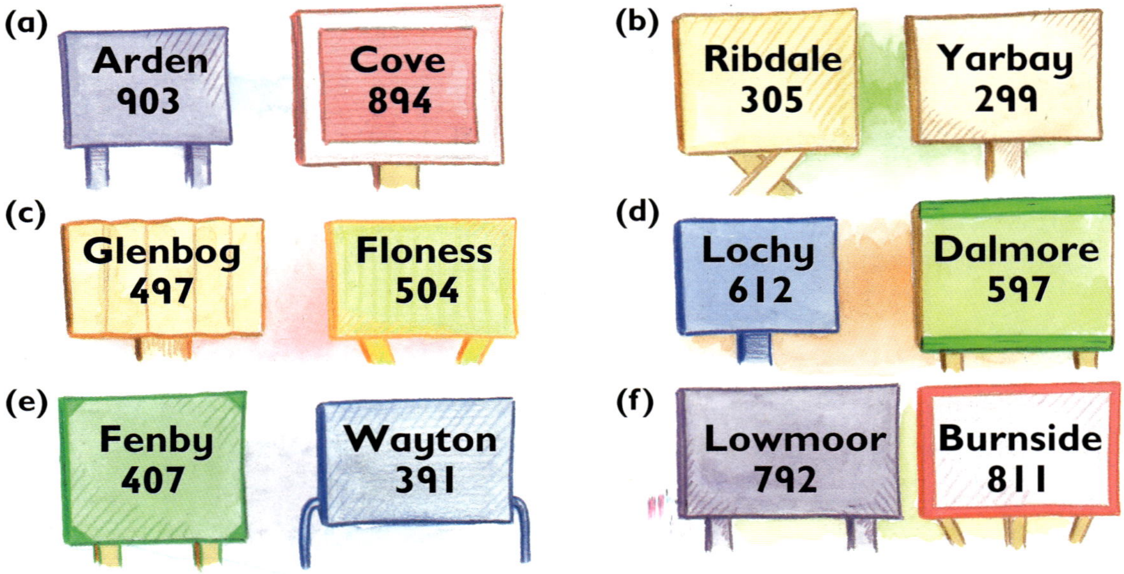


**3**

| | | | |
|---|---|---|---|
| **(a)** 802 - 693 | **(b)** 406 - 298 | **(c)** 905 - 398 | **(d)** 604 - 295 |
| **(e)** 703 - 486 | **(f)** 507 - 189 | **(g)** 314 - 196 | **(h)** 913 - 597 |
| **(i)** 505 - 289 | **(j)** 816 - 397 | **(k)** 615 - 398 | **(l)** 708 - 489 |

**4** Millburn's population is 17 greater than Deemouth's.
Newton's population is half of Millburn's.
How many people live in Newton?

**1** Copy and complete Ming's work.

**2** Use your answers in **question 1** to find

**(a)** 320 + 249 **(b)** 252 + 323
**(c)** 570 - 251 **(d)** 570 - 316

**3** Write two addition **and** two subtraction stories using each set of numbers.

**(a)** 627 340 967 **(b)** 323 783 460 **(c)** 550 987 437

**4** **(a)** Who has subtracted correctly? Check by **adding**.

**(b)** For each **correct** subtraction, write
- the addition you used to check
- another addition you **could** use to check.

**5** **(a)**  Check each subtraction by adding.

**(b)** Write each **correct** subtraction and **two** additions you could use to check it.

**1** How many fewer books about Travel than about History are there?

**2** Find the difference between the number of books in these sections of the library.

**(a)** SPORT 3997 books — FILMS AND TV 4004 books

**(b)** SCIENCE 2005 books — ART 1996 books

**(c)** COMPUTERS 1885 books — HOBBIES 2002 books

**(d)** ANIMALS 5012 books — HOMES 4898 books

**3**

| | | |
|---|---|---|
| **(a)** 8005 - 7989 | **(b)** 6011 - 5993 | **(c)** 1013 - 994 |
| **(d)** 9008 - 8987 | **(e)** 3001 - 2975 | **(f)** 7020 - 6991 |
| **(g)** 3004 - 2897 | **(h)** 4002 - 3898 | **(i)** 8010 - 7890 |
| **(j)** 5010 - 4940 | **(k)** 7001 - 6800 | **(l)** 4005 - 3750 |

**4** The library has 9015 Fiction books and 26 fewer Children's books. How many Children's books are there?

**5**

**(a)** 9003 - ■ = 5 **(b)** ■ - 5992 = 12

**(c)** 7002 - ■ = 106 **(d)** ■ - 890 = 130

# DESERT CAR RALLY

**1** The British car has travelled 4005 miles

The French car has travelled 1997 miles

How many more miles has the British car travelled?

**2** Find the difference between the number of miles travelled by these cars.

**(a)** German car: 995 miles — Dutch car: 3002 miles

**(b)** Italian car: 5008 miles — Spanish car: 2999 miles

**(c)** Swedish car: 4001 miles — Irish car: 991 miles

**(d)** Austrian car: 1998 miles — Danish car: 6004 miles

**3**

| | | |
|---|---|---|
| **(a)** 9002 – 5991 | **(b)** 7009 – 3994 | **(c)** 8004 – 6985 |
| **(d)** 5005 – 1989 | **(e)** 6007 – 4992 | **(f)** 9011 – 2993 |
| **(g)** 8001 – 4980 | **(h)** 7014 – 2990 | **(i)** 4007 – 985 |
| **(j)** 6030 – 3990 | **(k)** 9007 – 4950 | **(l)** 8020 – 1975 |

**4** The display shows how many miles the Australian car has travelled.

5008

The American car has travelled 29 miles fewer.
How many miles has the American car travelled?

1

How much more money has been raised for the Appeal by

**(a)** Sidburgh than Barnley
**(b)** Pipdale than Barnley
**(c)** Forsham than Barnley
**(d)** Sidburgh than Forsham
**(e)** Pipdale than Forsham
**(f)** Pipdale than Sidburgh?

**2**
**(a)** 3592 - 485
**(b)** 6114 - 931
**(c)** 7256 - 879
**(d)** 5463 - 2128
**(e)** 9706 - 1540
**(f)** 4377 - 2765
**(g)** 8730 - 4357
**(h)** 5627 - 2856
**(i)** 3064 - 1425
**(j)** 4371 - 2982
**(k)** 7153 - 5278
**(l)** 6050 - 3959

**3** A total of £6511 has been raised so far for the *Wildlife Garden Appeal.*

How much more money is needed to reach the TARGET of £9000?

**1** Subtract 768 from the difference beween 9074 and 8156.

**2** Use **two** of these numbers each time.

4018 562 3103 95

List **all** the differences you can make.

**3** Find the missing numbers.

(a) 931 – ■ = 746
(b) ■ – 257 = 429
(c) 6805 – ■ = 3528
(d) ■ – 4097 = 1673

**4** Find the missing **digits**.

(a) ■63 – 4▲2 = 521

(b) 5■26 – 190▲ = 3523

**5** The difference between two numbers is 3957. The smaller number is 898 less than 5000. What is the larger number?

**6** Which of these numbers do you **think** is the difference between 7260 and 1358?

6102 5910 5902 5112

Check using your calculator.

1 Tickets for *International Sportslinks* events are sold in **books of 100**.
How many tickets have been sold for each of these events?

**(a)** long jump 26 **(b)** triple jump 47 **(c)** high jump 58

**(d)** hurdles 132 **(e)** pole vault 180 **(f)** javelin 211

**(g)** marathon 263 **(h)** 400 metres 374 **(i)** 100 metres 509

2 What do you notice about your answers in question 1?

**3** **(a)** 100 × 238 = ■ **(b)** 100 × 96 = ■ **(c)** 341 × 100 = ■
**(d)** 100 × 16 = ■ **(e)** 100 × 107 = ■ **(f)** 54 × 100 = ■

**4** **(a)** 100 × ■ = 3500 **(b)** 100 × ■ = 12 300 **(c)** 100 × ■ = 1900
**(d)** ■ × 100 = 4100 **(e)** ■ × 100 = 9200 **(f)** ■ × 100 = 10 400

**5**

**Pool events**
**10 sheets of tickets**
**10 tickets on each sheet**

How many sheets and how many tickets were sold for these events?

**(a)** swimming – 63 books
**(b)** diving – 159 books

**1** Programmes for the events are packed in **boxes of 200**.
How many programmes are there for each of these events?

**(a)** rowing
80 boxes

**(b)** canoeing
30 boxes

**(c)** sailing
50 boxes

**(d)** water ski-ing
20 boxes

**(e)** surfing
90 boxes

**(f)** wind-surfing
60 boxes

**2** Explain how you found the answers in question **1**.

**3** **(a)** Multiply 10 by 200. **(b)** 40 multiplied by 200
**(c)** 70 times 200 **(d)** 200 times double 25

**4**

| | | | | | |
|---|---|---|---|---|---|
| **(a)** | 300 × 10 | **(b)** | 800 × 90 | **(c)** | 60 × 400 |
| **(d)** | 900 × 50 | **(e)** | 400 × 20 | **(f)** | 40 × 300 |
| **(g)** | 500 × 80 | **(h)** | 600 × 40 | **(i)** | 70 × 700 |
| **(j)** | 700 × 80 | **(k)** | 600 × 30 | **(l)** | 30 × 500 |

**5** **(a)** Multiply 500 by 60, then add 400.
**(b)** Find 70 muliplied by 400, then add 200.
**(c)** Find 30 times 900, then subtract 700.
**(d)** Multiply 50 by 600 and 20 by 800.
Add the two products.
**(e)** Find 80 multiplied by 600 and 40 multiplied by 900.
What is the difference between the two products?

**1** Find the cost **in Euros** of

(a) 7 　(b) 5 　(c) 10 　(d) 9 

(e) 6 　(f) 4 　(g) 8 　(h) 6 

(i) 9  and 7 　(j) 5  and 9 

(k) 8  and 4 　(l) 7  and 9 

**2**

| | | | |
|---|---|---|---|
| (a) $3 \times 8$ | (b) $4 \times 4$ | (c) $7 \times 5$ | (d) $9 \times 9$ |
| (e) $8 \times 5$ | (f) $6 \times 8$ | (g) $7 \times 9$ | (h) $8 \times 2$ |
| (i) $10 \times 10$ | (j) $0 \times 6$ | (k) $9 \times 4$ | (l) $7 \times 7$ |
| (m) $8 \times 9$ | (n) $7 \times 8$ | (o) $10 \times 7$ | (p) $9 \times 8$ |

**3**

| | | | |
|---|---|---|---|
| (a) $6 \times ■ = 42$ | (b) $9 \times ■ = 18$ | (c) $■ \times 8 = 80$ | (d) $■ \times 3 = 15$ |
| (e) $4 \times ■ = 0$ | (f) $5 \times ■ = 30$ | (g) $■ \times 6 = 24$ | (h) $■ \times 4 = 20$ |

**4** Maxine spent a total of €120.
She bought **two** kinds of souvenirs.

Which souvenirs and how many of each could she have bought?
Explain.

**1** How much would it cost to buy

(a) **4** 
(b) **10** 
(c) **8** 

(d) **7** 

(e) **9** 
(f) **6** 

(g) **10** 
(h) **3** 
(i) **4** 

(j) **3** 
(k) **7** 
(l) **5** 

**2** The Rocky Mountain Company prints 8 posters in one minute.

How many posters can they print in

(a) 5 minutes
(b) 9 minutes
(c) 3 minutes
(d) 8 minutes
(e) 10 minutes
(f) 6 minutes?

**3** Find the product of each pair of numbers.

(a) 5 10
(b) 4 7
(c) 8 4
(d) 3 0
(e) 7 9
(f) 7 5

**4** List pairs of numbers with a product of

(a) 12
(b) 20
(c) 36
(d) 40

**5** List **three** numbers with a product of 30.

**1** **(a)** When Wesley has 9 games, how many does Amy have?
**(b)** When Amy has 16 games, how many does Wesley have?

**2** How many games do they have **altogether** when
**(a)** Wesley has 7 **(b)** Amy has 10?

**3** Write True (T) or False (F).
**(a)** Jane has three times as many CDs as Terry.
**(b)** Terry has one third of the **total** number of CDs.
**(c)** When Terry has 5 CDs, Jane has 15.
**(d)** When Jane has 36 CDs, Terry has 9.

**4** The Music Club has 3 boys for every 2 girls.
There are 27 boys at the Club.
How many girls are there?

**5** The Dance Club has 5 times as many girls as boys.
There are 20 boys at the Club.
How many girls are there?

**6** The Games Club has 6 boys for every 4 girls.
There are 12 girls at the Club.
How many **children** are there?

**£1** can be exchanged for:

**2 Swiss Francs**

**3 Brazilian Real**

**4 New Zealand Dollars**

**9 South African Rand**

**1** How much money should each person receive?

**(a)**

**(b)**

**(c)**

**(d)**

**2** Exchange each of these amounts for

- Brazilian Real
- South African Rand.

**(a)** £42 **(b)** £53 **(c)** £83 **(d)** £65

**3** **(a)** $5 \times 74$ **(b)** $6 \times 58$ **(c)** $37 \times 8$ **(d)** $7 \times 92$
**(e)** $8 \times 29$ **(f)** $67 \times 7$ **(g)** $6 \times 86$ **(h)** $5 \times 99$

**4** **50p** can be exchanged for:

**7 Mexican Pesos**

**6 Danish Kroner**

How much money should Claire receive when she exchanges

**(a)** £33 for Danish Kroner **(b)** £47 for Mexican Pesos?

# International Trade Fair

**1** What is the cost of 20 of each?

**(a)** Maple Syrup **(b)** Coffee **(c)** Wool
**(d)** Cotton **(e)** Tea **(f)** Rice

**2** **(a)** $20 \times 12 = \square$ **(b)** $20 \times 19 = \square$ **(c)** $11 \times 20 = \square$
**(d)** $20 \times \square = 260$ **(e)** $\square \times 20 = 320$ **(f)** $20 \times \square = 400$

**3** How much did each person spend?

**(a)**

**(b)**

**(c)**

**(d)**

**(e)**

**(f)**

**4** **(a)** $19 \times 22$ **(b)** $21 \times 32$ **(c)** $23 \times 19$ **(d)** $21 \times 34$
**(e)** $19 \times 28$ **(f)** $26 \times 21$ **(g)** $19 \times 25$ **(h)** $21 \times 39$

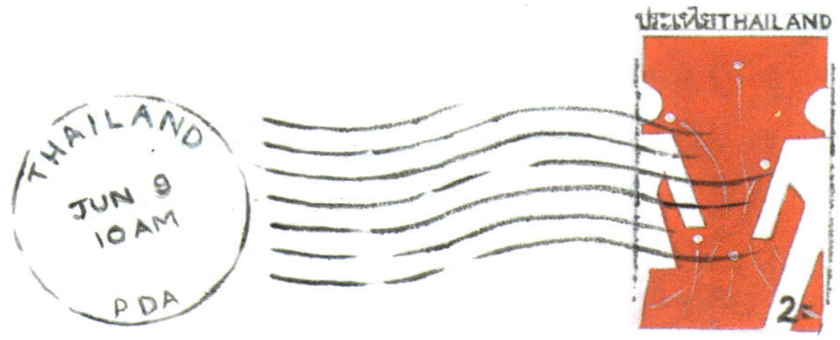


**1** (a) $5 \times 18$ (b) $5 \times 24$ (c) $32 \times 5$ (d) $15 \times 14$
(e) $15 \times 16$ (f) $18 \times 15$ (g) $25 \times 12$ (h) $25 \times 16$
(i) $18 \times 25$ (j) $46 \times 5$ (k) $45 \times 18$ (l) $14 \times 35$

**2** Which is greater and by how much?

(a) $15 \times 20$ or $25 \times 14$
(b) $35 \times 16$ or $45 \times 12$
(c) $5 \times 82$ or $25 \times 16$

**3** (a) $14 \times 13$ (b) $12 \times 22$ (c) $16 \times 21$ (d) $14 \times 11$
(e) $16 \times 17$ (f) $18 \times 13$ (g) $14 \times 24$ (h) $18 \times 17$
(i) $12 \times 38$ (j) $16 \times 29$ (k) $18 \times 11$ (l) $12 \times 19$

**4** Find the missing numbers.

(a) Multiply ■ by 12 and the product is 168.
(b) Multiply ■ by 16 and the product is 176.

**1** Copy and complete each example **to multiply by 50**.

| | | × 100 | | ÷ 2 | |
|---|---|---|---|---|---|
| (a) | 16 | → | 1600 | → | ▲ |
| (b) | 13 | → | ■ | → | ▲ |
| (c) | 18 | → | ■ | → | ▲ |
| (d) | 21 | → | ■ | → | ▲ |
| (e) | 24 | → | ■ | → | ▲ |
| (f) | 30 | → | ■ | → | ▲ |

**2** Multiply each number by 50.

**(a)** 28 **(b)** 22 **(c)** 15 **(d)** 36 **(e)** 44 **(f)** 67

**3** **(a)** $50 \times ■ = 2000$ **(b)** $■ \times 50 = 3800$ **(c)** $50 \times ■ = 4950$

**4** Copy and complete this doubles table for 25.

$1 \times 25 = ■$
$2 \times 25 = ■$
$4 \times 25 = ■$
$8 \times 25 = ■$

**5** Use your doubles table to find the missing numbers.

**(a)** $(1 \times 25) + (8 \times 25) = ■$
**(b)** $(2 \times 25) + (4 \times 25) = ■$
**(c)** $(4 \times 25) + (1 \times 25) = ■$
**(d)** $(8 \times 25) + (2 \times 25) = ■$
**(e)** $(8 \times 25) - (1 \times 25) = ■$
**(f)** $(4 \times 25) - (1 \times 25) = ■$

**6** **(a)** $11 \times 25$ **(b)** $13 \times 25$ **(c)** $15 \times 25$ **(d)** $20 \times 25$

**7** Make a doubles table for 16 and use it to find

**(a)** $6 \times 16$ **(b)** $9 \times 16$ **(c)** $14 \times 16$.

**1** How many litres of fuel are in

(a) 2 drums of Paraffin (b) 4 drums of Diesel (c) 3 drums of Oil
(d) 6 drums of Petrol (e) 7 drums of Oil (f) 9 drums of Petrol?

**2** Which holds more

(a) 3 drums of Paraffin or 2 drums of Diesel
(b) 5 drums of Oil or 8 drums of Paraffin
(c) 4 drums of Petrol or 6 drums of Oil
(d) 9 drums of Diesel or 7 drums of Petrol?

**3** How much does Mr Brown pay for

(a) 8 headlights (b) 3 fuel tanks (c) 5 sets of brakes?

**4** Which of these cost **between** £1500 and £1750?

(a) 5 exhausts (b) 9 windscreens (c) 2 fuel tanks
(d) 6 tyres (e) 3 headlights (f) 4 sets of brakes

**5** Mr Brown has £3500 to spend.
Is it possible for him to buy 4 windscreens, 4 headlights and 4 sets of brakes? Explain.

# Coral Beach Watersports Centre

**1** What does the Watersports Centre pay for

**(a)** 23 masks  **(b)** 16 air tanks  **(c)** 52 pairs of flippers
**(d)** 44 torches  **(e)** 37 watches?

**2** How much money did the Watersports Centre earn from these courses?

**(a)** parascending ➔ 13 people
**(b)** wind-surfing ➔ 32 people
**(c)** scuba-diving ➔ 24 people
**(d)** dinghy-sailing ➔ 28 people
**(e)** water-skiing ➔ 46 people

**Coral Beach Watersports Centre**
**Training Courses**

| | |
|---|---|
| scuba-diving | £74 |
| parascending | £95 |
| wind-surfing | £43 |
| dinghy-sailing | £51 |
| water-skiing | £39 |

**3**

**(a)** $66 \times 55$  **(b)** $58 \times 71$  **(c)** $94 \times 26$  **(d)** $49 \times 53$
**(e)** $87 \times 41$  **(f)** $75 \times 67$  **(g)** $59 \times 92$  **(h)** $83 \times 64$

# Monster Party

Ricky: I saved 75p every week for one year.

Gita: I saved 60p every week for a year and a half.

**1** How much money did each child save for the party?

**2** Ricky will be 10 years old on his birthday.
Has he lived for more than 90 000 hours? Explain.

**3** There are 125 children at the Monster Party.
Every child receives one of each of these items.

(a) 

(b) 

(c) 

(d) 

Find the total cost for each item.

**4**

| Birthday Cake | |
|---|---|
| Icing | 375 g |
| Flour | 650 g |
| Butter | 225 g |
| Sultanas | 125 g |
| Cherries | 95 g |
| Sugar | 160 g |

45 Birthday cakes are baked for the party.
Find the total weight of each ingredient used.

**5** Solve these Puzzle Cards from the Birthday Bags.

**(a)** Use these digits to make a two-digit number and a three-digit number which give

- the largest possible product
- the smallest possible product.

1 2 3 4 5

**(b)** Find the missing number.

$15 \times 60 + \blacksquare = 960$

**(c)** Which number, multiplied by **itself**, gives a product of 625?

**1** Sandie makes 24 cheese sandwiches.
Each tray holds 8 sandwiches.
How many trays can she fill?

**2** How many trays can Sandie fill with these sandwiches?

**(a)** 

35 sandwiches, 7 in each tray.

**(b)** 

72 sandwiches, 9 in each tray.

**(c)** 

40 sandwiches, 5 in each tray.

**(d)** 

70 sandwiches, 10 in each tray.

**(e)** 

20 sandwiches, 4 in each tray.

**(f)** 

18 sandwiches, 6 in each tray.

**3** **(a)** Divide 54 by 9.
**(b)** Share 14 equally among 7.
**(c)** Zero divided by 3
**(d)** How many tens make 100?
**(e)** Divide 72 by 8.
**(f)** 20 divided equally among 5
**(g)** Half of 14
**(h)** How many groups of six are in 30?

**4** **(a)** $7 \div 7 = \blacksquare$ **(b)** $80 \div 10 = \blacksquare$ **(c)** $56 \div 8 = \blacksquare$ **(d)** $28 \div 4 = \blacksquare$
**(e)** $\blacksquare \div 9 = 9$ **(f)** $\blacksquare \div 5 = 0$ **(g)** $\blacksquare \div 10 = 4$ **(h)** $\blacksquare \div 8 = 4$
**(i)** $42 \div \blacksquare = 6$ **(j)** $45 \div \blacksquare = 5$ **(k)** $12 \div \blacksquare = 2$ **(l)** $80 \div \blacksquare = 10$

**5** How many **free** sandwiches will Sandie's Special Offer give with
**(a)** 24 sandwiches **(b)** 54 sandwiches
**(c)** 36 sandwiches **(d)** 60 sandwiches?

**1** Divide the sandwiches equally among the trays.

**(a)**

10 trays

**(b)**

6 trays

**(c)**

9 trays

**(d)**

5 trays

**(e)**

3 trays

**2** **(a)** $\frac{18}{9} = \square$ **(b)** $\frac{50}{10} = \square$ **(c)** $\frac{0}{6} = \square$ **(d)** $\frac{28}{7} = \square$

**(e)** $\frac{\square}{2} = 9$ **(f)** $\frac{\square}{9} = 4$ **(g)** $\frac{\square}{4} = 1$ **(h)** $\frac{\square}{10} = 2$

**(i)** $\frac{27}{\square} = 3$ **(j)** $\frac{90}{\square} = 10$ **(k)** $\frac{48}{\square} = 8$ **(l)** $\frac{90}{\square} = 10$

**3** How many pickles can you buy when you spend
**(a)** 21p **(b)** 63p **(c)** 49p **(d)** 70p?

**4** How many sauces can you buy when you spend
**(a)** 48p **(b)** 16p **(c)** 40p **(d)** 64p?

**5** Tom bought **one third** as many pickles as Alexa.
Together their pickles cost 56p.
How many pickles did they each buy?

1 Simon Smith orders 300 address labels in **strips of 10.**

How many strips does he order?

**2** How many strips of 10 can be made with

**(a)** 500 labels **(b)** 2000 labels
**(c)** 4600 labels **(d)** 7300 labels?

**3** **(a)** ■ ÷ 10 = 80 **(b)** ■ ÷ 10 = 600 **(c)** ■ ÷ 10 = 250 **(d)** ■ ÷ 10 = 940

**4** Amy Arnott orders 600 address labels in **sheets of 100.**

How many sheets does she order?

**5** How many sheets of 100 can be made with

**(a)** 400 labels **(b)** 9000 labels
**(c)** 1800 labels **(d)** 8700 labels?

**6** **(a)** ■ ÷ 100 = 9 **(b)** ■ ÷ 100 = 40 **(c)** ■ ÷ 100 = 59 **(d)** ■ ÷ 100 = 31

**7** Martin Moore orders 7000 address labels in **packets of 1000.**

How many packets does he order?

**8** How many packets of 1000 can be made with

**(a)** 5000 labels **(b)** 8000 labels
**(c)** 3000 labels **(d)** 9000 labels?

**9**
**(a)** 200 ÷ 10 = ■ **(b)** 4000 ÷ 1000 = ■ **(c)** 700 ÷ 100 = ■
**(d)** 1700 ÷ 10 = ■ **(e)** 3000 ÷ 100 = ■ **(f)** 1000 ÷ 1000 = ■
**(g)** 6200 ÷ 100 = ■ **(h)** 8800 ÷ 10 = ■ **(i)** 9800 ÷ ■ = 98
**(j)** 6000 ÷ ■ = 6 **(k)** 5200 ÷ ■ = 520 **(l)** 4300 ÷ ■ = 43

**1** **(a)** List all the balloon numbers which divide exactly by 4.

**(b)** Divide the **last two digits** of each number on your list by 4. What do you notice?

**(c)** Describe a quick way to find if a number divides exactly by 4.

**(d)** Use your quick way to find which of these numbers divide exactly by 4.

**2**

Which of these are leap years?

**(a)**

**(b)**

**(c)**

**Investigations File**

**3** Write a fact about the **last digit** of a number that divides exactly by

**(a)** 10 **(b)** 5 **(c)** 2

**4** Write a fact about the **last two digits** of a number that divides exactly by 100.

**1** For each calculation, use the numbers to write another three multiplication or division stories.

**(a)** $56 \div 7 = 8$ **(b)** $6 \times 9 = 54$ **(c)** $150 \div 6 = 25$
**(d)** $10 \times 60 = 600$ **(e)** $94 \div 2 = 47$ **(f)** $4 \times 26 = 104$
**(g)** $221 \div 13 = 17$ **(h)** $12 \times 23 = 276$ **(i)** $770 \div 35 = 22$

**2**

For each set of numbers, write two multiplications **and** two divisions.

**(a)** 42 7 6 **(b)** 20 4 80 **(c)** 5 55 11

**(d)** 300 10 30 **(e)** 25 450 18 **(f)** 19 15 285

**3** Use the numbers 27, 43 and **one other number** to write four multiplications or divisions.

**1** Check Myra's answers by **multiplying**.
Correct any that are wrong.

**Name:** Myra

(a) 168 ÷ 7 = 24 (b) 288 ÷ 9 = 31

(c) 324 ÷ 12 = 27 (d) 352 ÷ 8 = 44

(e) 208 ÷ 13 = 15 (f) 266 ÷ 14 = 19

(g) 735 ÷ 21 = 33 (h) 782 ÷ 17 = 45

(i) 676 ÷ 26 = 26 (j) 1520 ÷ 40 = 38

**2** Copy and complete each division and write a **multiplication** that can be used to check it.

**(a)** 222 ÷ 6 = ■ **(b)** 162 ÷ ■ = 18
**(c)** ■ ÷ 15 = 33 **(d)** 517 ÷ 11 = ■
**(e)** 525 ÷ ■ = 25 **(f)** ■ ÷ 28 = 30
**(g)** 924 ÷ ■ = 22 **(h)** 1568 ÷ 32 = ■
**(i)** ■ ÷ 48 = 48 **(j)** 2160 ÷ ■ = 54

**3** Which two box numbers divide to give

**(a)** 20 **(b)** 30
**(c)** a number on **another** box
**(d)** a number that is on one of the two boxes?

**1** Oliver's red apple orchard has 120 trees in rows of 8.
How many rows of red apple trees are there?

**2** How many rows of trees are in these orchards?

| | Green apple | Pear | Red cherry | Black cherry | Plum |
|---|---|---|---|---|---|
| **Number of trees** | 117 | 133 | 108 | 153 | 144 |
| **Number in each row** | 9 | 7 | 6 | 9 | 8 |

**3** **(a)** 105 ÷ 7 **(b)** 108 ÷ 9 **(c)** 152 ÷ 8 **(d)** 144 ÷ 9

**4** Oliver grows 184 strawberry plants in 8 equal rows.
How many plants are in each row?

**5** These bushes are planted in equal rows.
How many bushes are in each row?

**(a)**

7 rows

**(b)**

9 rows

**(c)**

4 rows

**(d)** 117 blackcurrant - in 3 rows **(e)** 112 bramble - in 2 rows
**(f)** 265 gooseberry - in 5 rows **(g)** 450 loganberry - in 6 rows
**(h)** 752 bilberry - in 8 rows **(i)** 616 blueberry - in 7 rows

**6** **(a)** 452 ÷ 4 **(b)** 354 ÷ 3 **(c)** 912 ÷ 8 **(d)** 702 ÷ 6
**(e)** 648 ÷ 3 **(f)** 860 ÷ 4 **(g)** 663 ÷ 3 **(h)** 456 ÷ 2
**(i)** 878 ÷ 2 **(j)** 972 ÷ 3 **(k)** 765 ÷ 5 **(l)** 944 ÷ 4

**1** Oliver divides baskets of fruit equally amoung his trailers.
How many baskets are on each trailer and how many are left over?

| | Red apples | Green apples | Pears | Plums | Black cherries | Red cherries |
|---|---|---|---|---|---|---|
| **Number of baskets** | 114 | 169 | 124 | 131 | 143 | 118 |
| **Number of trailers** | 8 | 9 | 7 | 8 | 9 | 6 |

**2** Trays of fruit are packed in boxes and sent to the supermarkets.

How many boxes can be **filled** with trays?

How many trays are left over?

| | Red apples | Green apples | Pears | Plums | Black cherries | Red cherries |
|---|---|---|---|---|---|---|
| **Number of trays** | 118 | 174 | 157 | 195 | 220 | 175 |
| **Trays in each box** | 5 | 7 | 3 | 4 | 6 | 2 |

**3** **(a)** 564 ÷ 5 **(b)** 818 ÷ 7 **(c)** 929 ÷ 7 **(d)** 770 ÷ 6
**(e)** 907 ÷ 4 **(f)** 709 ÷ 3 **(g)** 943 ÷ 2 **(h)** 857 ÷ 3

**4** Oliver divides 151 baskets of fruit amoung 8 trailers.
One trailer has 7 baskets more than each of the others.

How many baskets of fruit are on each trailer?

**1** How many trays are needed for 116 apples when each tray holds

(a) 8 apples (b) 9 apples

(c) 6 apples (d) 7 apples?

**2** How many trays can be **filled** with these fruits?

| | Apples | Pears | Cherries | Plums |
|---|---|---|---|---|
| **Number of fruits** | 137 | 257 | 219 | 379 |
| **Number in each tray** | 2 | 3 | 4 | 5 |

**3** (a) Four baskets of strawberries cost £13. What is the cost of each basket?

(b) Find the cost of one basket of each type of fruit.

**4** How much, **to the nearest pound,** does each supermarket pay Oliver for one box of fruit?

| | Total paid | Boxes of fruit |
|---|---|---|
| **Supersave** | £25 | 3 |
| **Magico** | £62 | 7 |
| **Snips** | £49 | 6 |
| **Cost-u-less** | £73 | 9 |
| **Savershop** | £69 | 8 |

**1** What fraction of each shape is coloured?

**(a)**

**(b)**

**(c)**
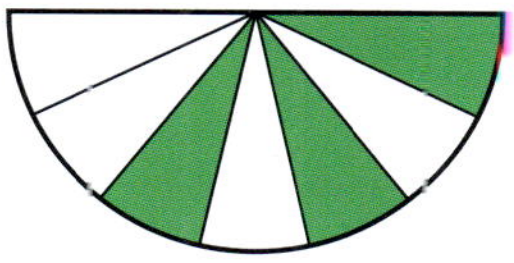

**(d)**
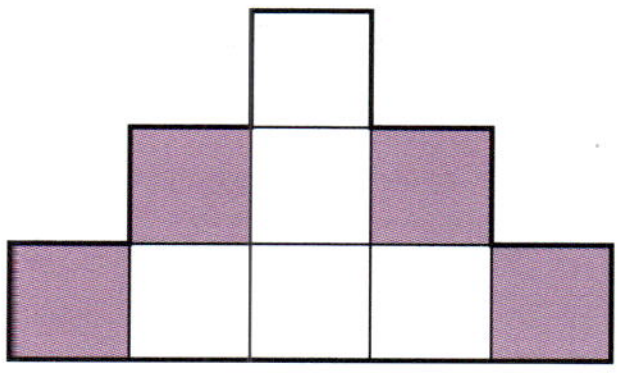

**(e)**
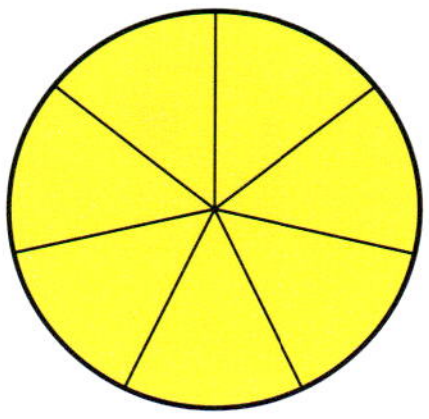

**(f)**
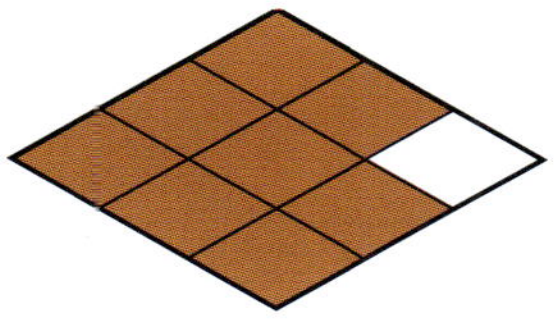

**(g)**
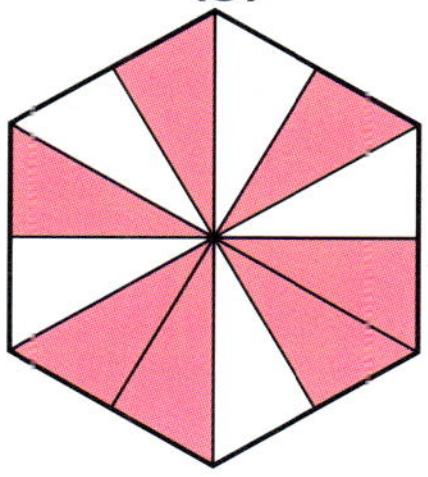

**(h)**

**2** How many shapes in each set are coloured?

**(a)**
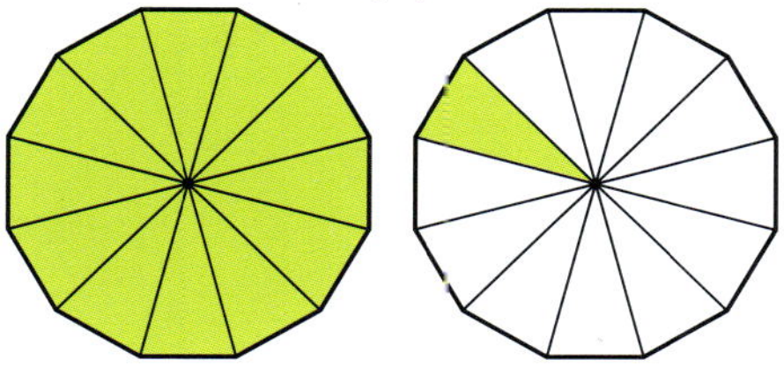

**(b)**
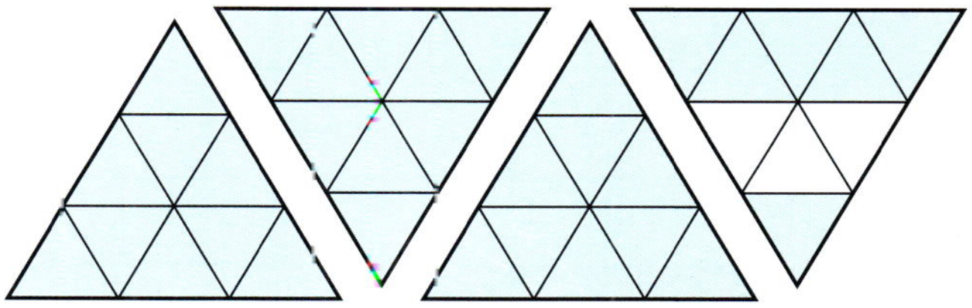

**(c)**
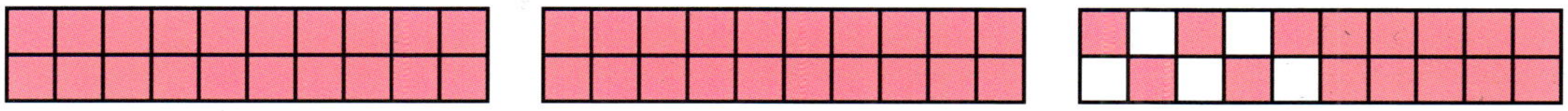

**3** Write as an improper fraction.

**(a)** $2\frac{4}{20}$ **(b)** $3\frac{2}{7}$ **(c)** $4\frac{7}{9}$ **(d)** $2\frac{10}{12}$ **(e)** $1\frac{19}{20}$ **(f)** $5\frac{5}{9}$

**4** Write as a mixed number.

**(a)** $\frac{64}{9}$ **(b)** $\frac{61}{20}$ **(c)** $\frac{83}{9}$ **(d)** $\frac{19}{7}$ **(e)** $\frac{100}{20}$ **(f)** $\frac{50}{12}$

**1** Copy and complete each equal fractions story.

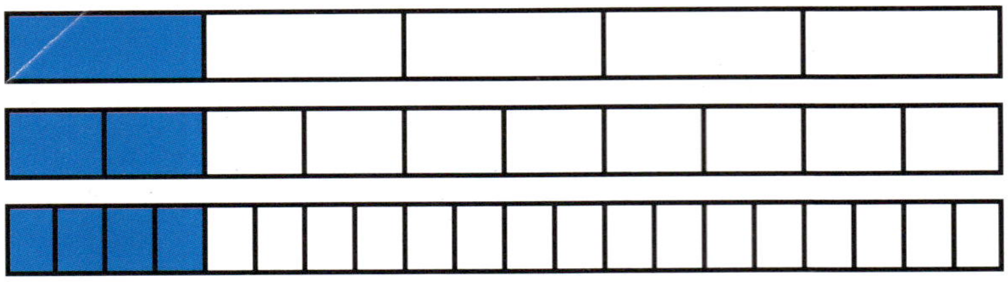

(a) $\frac{\square}{5} = \frac{\square}{10} = \frac{\square}{\square}$

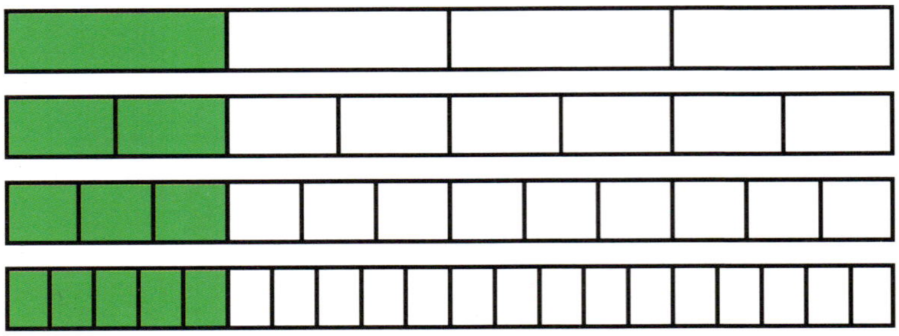

(b) $\frac{1}{\square} = \frac{\square}{8} = \frac{3}{\square} = \frac{\square}{\square}$

(c) $\frac{\square}{3} = \frac{\square}{\square} = \frac{\square}{9} = \frac{\square}{\square}$

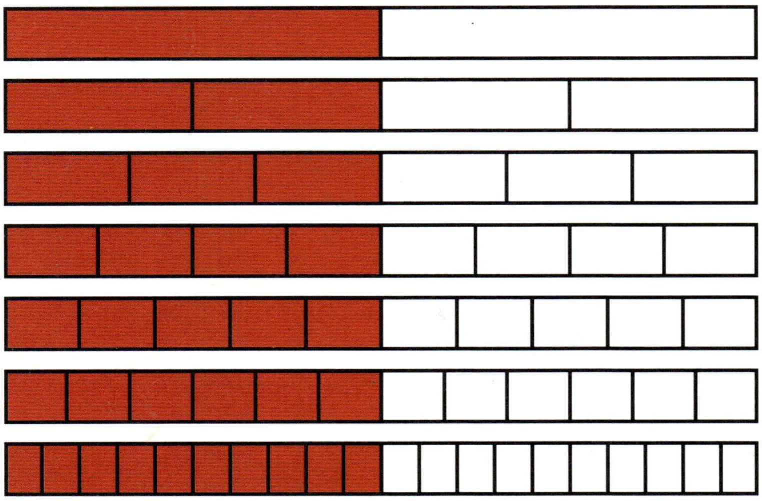

(d) $\frac{1}{2} = \frac{\square}{\square} = \frac{\square}{\square} = \frac{\square}{\square} = \frac{\square}{\square} = \frac{\square}{\square} = \frac{\square}{\square}$

**1** Copy and complete.

(a) One eighth is ___ of one quarter.

(b) One tenth is half of one ___.

(c) One ___ is half of one third.

(d) One twelfth is half of one ___ .

(e) One ___ is half of one tenth.

**2**

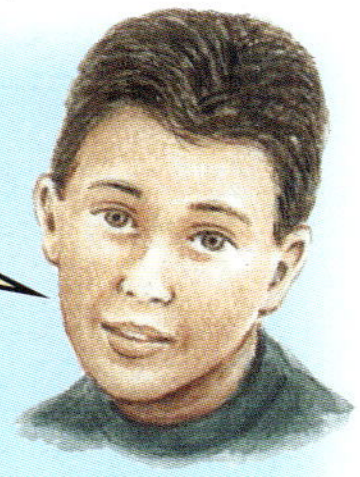


Write < or > between each pair of fractions.

(a) $\frac{1}{5}$ and $\frac{1}{10}$ (b) $\frac{1}{20}$ and $\frac{1}{12}$ (c) $\frac{1}{8}$ and $\frac{1}{9}$ (d) $\frac{1}{9}$ and $\frac{1}{12}$

(e) $\frac{1}{4}$ and $\frac{1}{5}$ (f) $\frac{1}{8}$ and $\frac{1}{7}$ (g) $\frac{1}{6}$ and $\frac{1}{5}$ (h) $\frac{1}{9}$ and $\frac{1}{10}$

**3** Find **three** fractions

(a) greater than one half (b) less than one half.

**4** Write a fraction

(a) smaller than one tenth (b) greater than one third.

**5** List the numbers in order.

(a) Start with the largest. $\frac{1}{2}$ $1\frac{1}{2}$ $2$ $\frac{1}{4}$ $1\frac{1}{4}$ $\frac{3}{4}$

(b) Start with the smallest. $\frac{1}{3}$ $3$ $1\frac{1}{6}$ $\frac{2}{3}$ $1\frac{3}{6}$ $\frac{5}{6}$

**6** Copy this part of a number line:

Label the positions of $\frac{11}{12}$ $\frac{1}{6}$ $\frac{1}{3}$ $\frac{1}{2}$ $\frac{1}{4}$

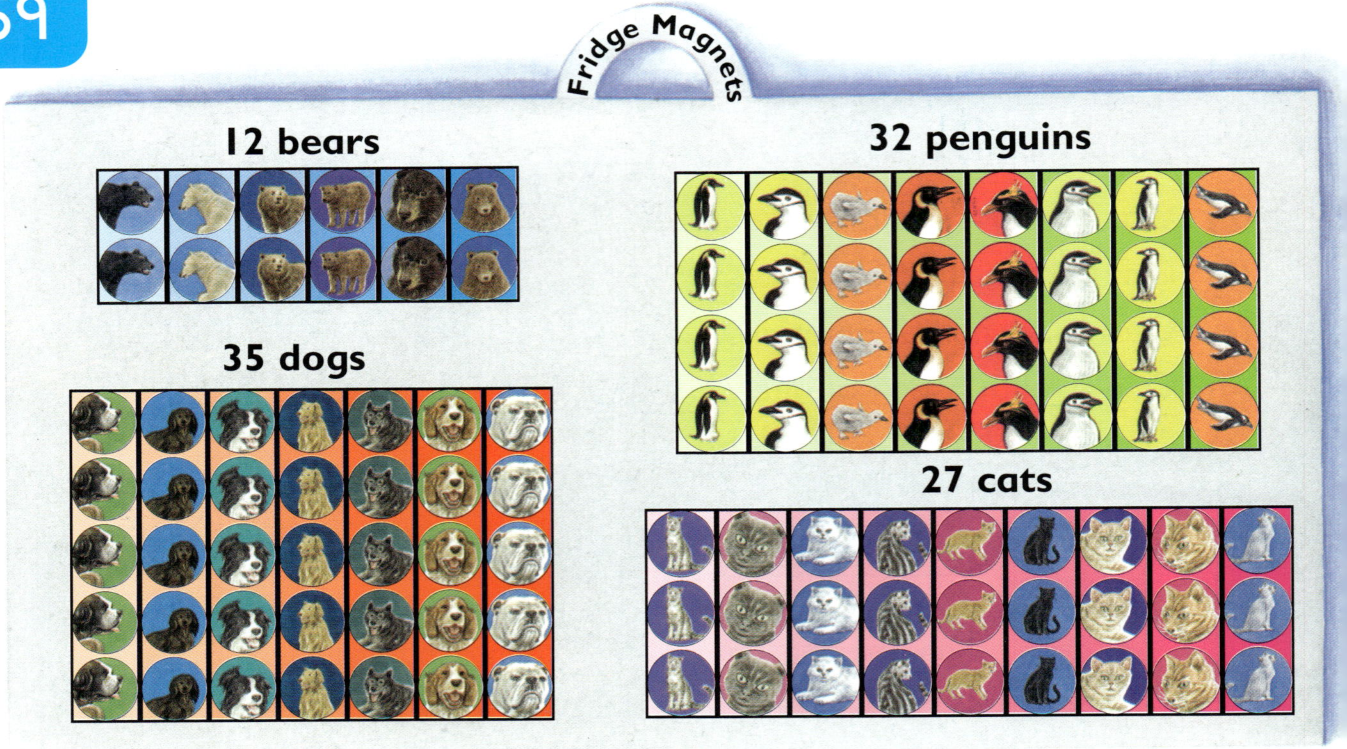


**1** Find (a) $\frac{1}{6}$ of the bears (b) $\frac{1}{8}$ of the penguins

(c) $\frac{1}{7}$ of the dogs (d) $\frac{1}{9}$ of the cats

**2** (a) $\frac{1}{8}$ of 72 (b) $\frac{1}{6}$ of 42 (c) $\frac{1}{9}$ of 90 (d) one seventh of 56

(e) $\frac{1}{6}$ of 6 (f) $\frac{1}{8}$ of 64 (g) $\frac{1}{7}$ of 21 (h) one ninth of 63

(i) $\frac{1}{7}$ of 63 (j) $\frac{1}{9}$ of 72 (k) $\frac{1}{6}$ of 60 (l) on eighth of 8

(m) $\frac{1}{5}$ of 45 (n) $\frac{1}{7}$ of 28 (o) $\frac{1}{9}$ of 54 (p) one sixth of 30

**3**

I bought six whale magnets.

Jo bought one eighth of the magnets on the whales card.
How many whale magnets were on the card?

**1** Find each fraction of the hearts.

**(a)** $\frac{3}{10}$ **(b)** $\frac{9}{10}$ **(c)** $\frac{3}{4}$

**2** Find each fraction of the roses.

**(a)** $\frac{4}{5}$ **(b)** $\frac{2}{5}$ **(c)** $\frac{2}{3}$

**3** **(a)** $\frac{2}{10}$ of 70 **(b)** $\frac{3}{5}$ of 10 **(c)** $\frac{2}{3}$ of 24 **(d)** three quarters of 20

**(e)** $\frac{4}{5}$ of 50 **(f)** $\frac{7}{10}$ of 90 **(g)** $\frac{3}{5}$ of 25 **(h)** two thirds of 9

**(i)** $\frac{3}{4}$ of 100 **(j)** $\frac{4}{10}$ of 800 **(k)** $\frac{8}{10}$ of 300 **(l)** five tenths of 600

**4** Write

- in centimetres

**(a)** $\frac{6}{10}$m **(b)** $\frac{9}{10}$m **(c)** $\frac{5}{10}$m

- in pence

**(a)** £$\frac{2}{10}$ **(b)** £$\frac{4}{10}$ **(c)** £$\frac{7}{10}$

**5** Write **(a)** $\frac{5}{10}$ km in metres **(b)** $\frac{2}{10}$ $\ell$ in millilitres **(c)** $\frac{5}{10}$ kg in grams

**6** What fraction is

**(a)** 30 cm of 1 metre **(b)** 80p of £1 **(c)** 200 m of 1 kilometre
**(d)** 800 g of 1 kilogram **(e)** 400 ml of 1 litre **(f)** 750 g of 1 kilogram?

**1** Workers at *Peter's Petfoods* give $\frac{1}{100}$ of their bonus to the charity *Petcare*. How much does each of these workers give to *Petcare*?

| Bonus | Bonus | Bonus | Bonus |
|---|---|---|---|
| **Adam £400** | **Baka £700** | **Cara £1000** | **Damon £1300** |

**2** **(a)** $\frac{1}{100}$ of 300 **(b)** $\frac{1}{100}$ of 800 **(c)** $\frac{1}{100}$ of 100 **(d)** $\frac{1}{100}$ of 500

**(e)** $\frac{1}{100}$ of 2000 **(f)** $\frac{1}{100}$ of 9000 **(g)** $\frac{1}{100}$ of 6000 **(h)** $\frac{1}{100}$ of 8600

**(i)** $\frac{1}{100}$ of 3900 **(j)** $\frac{1}{100}$ of 6400 **(k)** $\frac{1}{100}$ of 4100 **(l)** $\frac{1}{100}$ of 5800

**3** Write

- in centimetres

**(a)** $\frac{52}{100}$ m **(b)** $\frac{35}{100}$ m **(c)** $\frac{90}{100}$ m

- in pence

**(d)** £$\frac{17}{100}$ **(e)** £$\frac{24}{100}$ **(f)** £$\frac{10}{100}$

**4** What fraction is
**(a)** 68 p of £1 **(b)** 99 p of £1 **(c)** 1 cm of 1 metre **(d)** 50 cm of 1 metre?

**5** Write **(a)** $\frac{1}{100}$ km in metres **(b)** $\frac{1}{100}$ kg in grams **(c)** $\frac{1}{100}$ ℓ in millilitres

**6** How much was the **bonus** earned by each of these workers at *Peter's Petfoods*?

**1** Which space ship has the same number as

**(a)** 7·8 **(b)** $2\frac{7}{10}$ **(c)** thirty-four tenths

**(d)** 0·7 **(e)** $17\frac{2}{10}$ **(f)** four and three tenths?

**2** Copy and complete each sequence.

**(a)** 0·2, 0·4, 0·6, ___, ___, ___

**(b)** 2·6, 2·2, 1·8, ___, ___, ___

**(c)** 6·7, 6·4, 6·1, ___, ___, ___

**(d)** 2·4, 3·0, ___, 4·2 , ___, ___

**(e)** 10·5, 10·1 ___, ___, ___, 8·5

**(f)** 1·4, ___, ___, 2·9, ___, 3·9

**3** Write the number between:

**(a)** 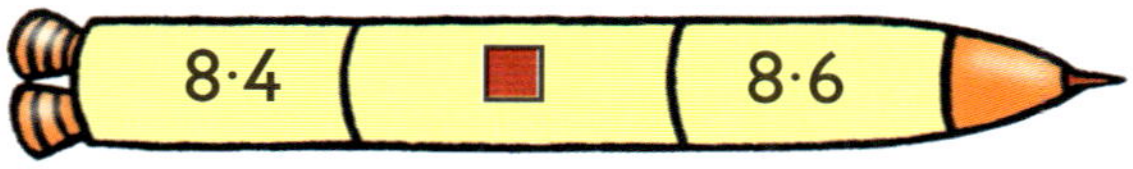


**(b)** 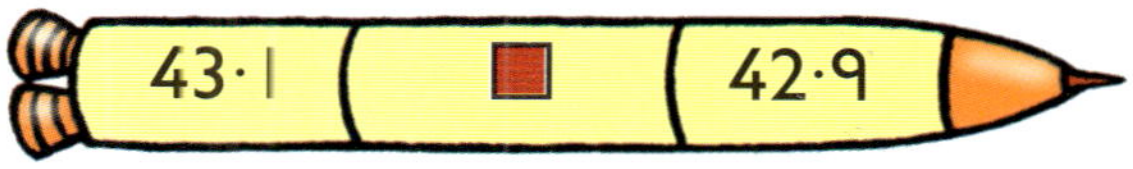


**(c)** 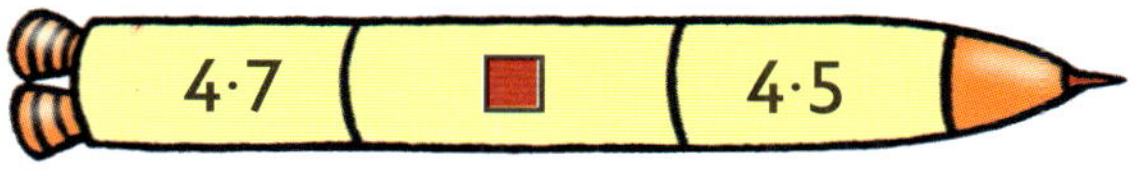


**(d)** 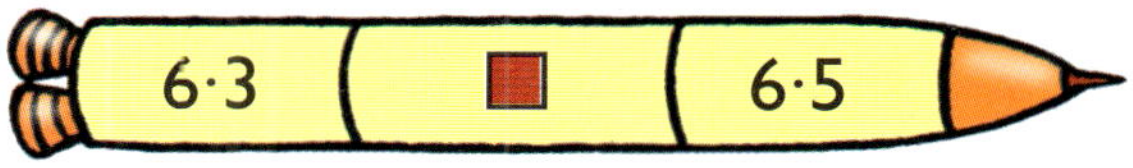


**4** Write **a** number between:

**(a)** 3·6  4·0

**(b)** 143  143·5

**(c)** 9·6  6·9

**(d)** 15·4  13·0

**(e)** 71·4  80

**(f)** 1  2·5

**1** Write the value of each **red** digit.

(a) **1** 3·7 (b) 4 **6**·5 (c) 6 2·**2**

(d) 3 **3**·3 (e) 5 8·**6** (f) **2** 9·4

**2** Write True (T) or False (F).

(a) 9·0 > 0·9 (b) 34·0 > 340 (c) 60·3 < 63·0

(d) $\frac{81}{10} > \frac{18}{10}$ (e) $4\frac{7}{10} < 7\frac{4}{10}$ (f) 9·3 < 3·9

**3** Write the smallest number.

(a) 2·3 3·2 23 (b) $64\frac{1}{10}$ 64 64·6

(c) 4·1 $1\frac{1}{10}$ 1·4 (d) 155 55·1 15·5

**4** List the numbers in order.

- Start with the **smallest**.

(a) 3·8 3·0 4·3 3·4 (b) 19·0 1·9 10·9 9·1

- Start with the **largest**.

(c) 2·5 $3\frac{5}{10}$ $2\frac{7}{10}$ 3·7 (d) 4·0 $\frac{4}{10}$ 14·0 $\frac{14}{10}$

**5**

Which space pod number is nearest to

(a) 5 (b) 3 (c) 2 (d) 6 (e) 1?

**6** Round to the **nearest whole number**.

(a) 6·8 (b) 3·6 (c) 6·3 (d) 10·4 (e) 17·9
(f) 55·2 (g) 29·7 (h) 234·1 (i) 749·0 (j) 199·5

**1** How many kg altogether of moonrocks did each robot pack?

**(a)** 0·6 kg, 0·2 kg **(b)** 0·3 kg, 0·5 kg **(c)** 0·1 kg, 0·7 kg

**(d)** 0·3 kg, 0·3 kg **(e)** 0·2 kg, 0·4 kg, 0·3 kg **(f)** 0·5 kg, 0·1 kg, 0·4 kg

**2** Double each number.

**(a)** 0·4 **(b)** 0·2 **(c)** 0·5 **(d)** 0·7 **(e)** 0·9

**3** **(a)** 0·7 + 0·3 **(b)** 0·6 + 0·7 **(c)** 0·8 + 0·9 **(d)** 0·5 + 0·9
**(e)** 0·7 + 0·8 **(f)** 0·9 + 0·6 **(g)** 0·6 + 0·5 **(h)** 0·8 + 0·4

**4** Add. **(a)** 0·3 + 1·5 **(b)** 0·6 + 4·3 **(c)** 0·9 + 5·1

**5** Increase **(a)** 2·8 by 0·5 **(b)** 3·9 by 0·4 **(c)** 1·3 by 0·8.

**6**

**(a)** 0·7 + ■ **(b)** 0·1 + ■
**(c)** ■ + 0·5 **(d)** ■ + 0·2
**(e)** 0·4 + 0·5 + ■ **(f)** 0·2 + ■ + 0·5

**7** Find the missing numbers.

**(a)** ■ + ▲ = 1 **(b)** ■ + ▲ + ◆ = 1
**(c)** ■ + ▲ < 1 **(d)** ■ + ▲ + ◆ < 1

**1** Find each total volume of asteroid acid.

(a) 3·5 ℓ 2·2 ℓ (b) 1·6 ℓ 4·3 ℓ (c) 6·5 ℓ 3·4 ℓ

(d) 4·1 ℓ 1·7 ℓ (e) 2·4 ℓ 5·3 ℓ (f) 6·2 ℓ 1·8 ℓ

**2** Double.

(a) 2·3 (b) 1·4 (c) 4·6 (d) 3·9 (e) 2·8

**3** (a) 7·7 + 1·2 (b) 5·5 + 2·5 (c) 5·8 + 2·7 (d) 3·8 + 3·4
(e) 2·2 + 4·9 (f) 6·9 + 2·8 (g) 2·5 + 1·8 (h) 2·6 + 4·7
(i) 7·3 + 7·9 (j) 9·7 + 4·4 (k) 5·7 + 5·7 (l) 8·6 + 6·8

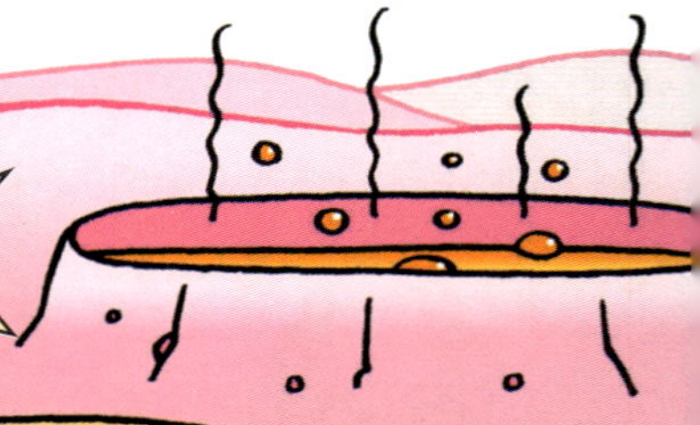

**Find the missing numbers.**

**4** (a) 2·6 + ■ = 3 (b) 4·1 + ■ = 5 (c) 5·4 + ■ = 6
(d) ■ + 6·3 = 7 (e) ■ + 9·7 = 10 (f) ■ + 7·8 = 8

**5** (a) ■ + ▲ = 6·8 (b) ■ + ▲ = 10·2 (c) ■ + ▲ = 13·5
(d) ■ + ▲ + ◆ = 7·6 (e) ■ + ▲ + ◆ = 8·3

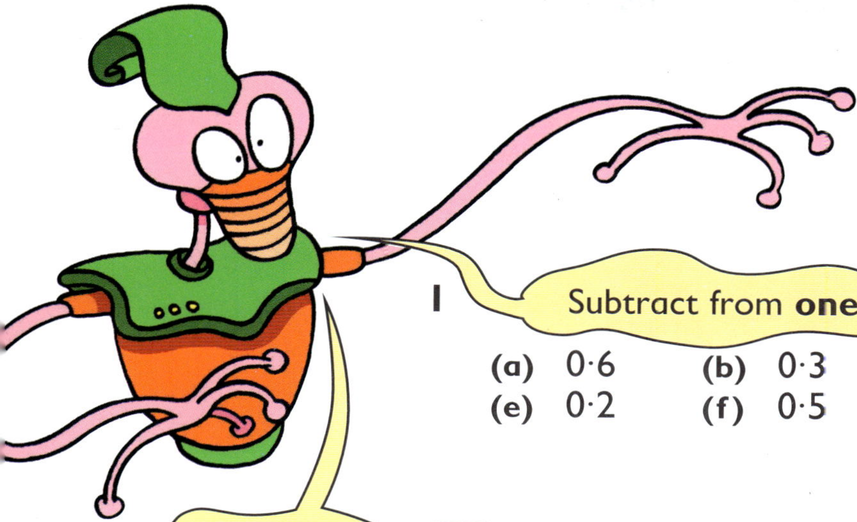

1 Subtract from **one**.

(a) 0·6 (b) 0·3 (c) 0·8 (d) 0·1
(e) 0·2 (f) 0·5 (g) 0·7 (h) 0·4

2 Subtract from **ten**.

(a) 3·4 (b) 7·3 (c) 1·2 (d) 5·7 (e) 2·9 (f) 4·5

3 (a) 5·6 − 0·4 (b) 6·7 − 0·6 (c) 9·9 − 1·7 (d) 10·8 − 5·5
(e) 7·5 − 6·2 (f) 8·1 − 4·0 (g) 6·0 − 5·0 (h) 3·0 − 1·9

4

Find the difference between the fuel loads of these spaceships.

(a) blue and yellow (b) orange and blue (c) yellow and orange
(d) purple and green (e) red and purple (f) orange and green

5 (a) 7·4 − 0·6 (b) 10·6 − 0·9 (c) 5·2 − 3·5 (d) 6·3 − 1·4
(e) 3·1 − 1·9 (f) 9·2 − 5·3 (g) 11·5 − 9·7 (h) 20·4 − 19·8

**1** How many spacewarps did *ALPHA* travel altogether?

**2** **(a)** 63·2 + 25·6 **(b)** 44·1 + 32·8 **(c)** 81·0 + 10·7 **(d)** 16·5 + 53·5
**(e)** 35·6 + 46·2 **(f)** 59·3 +27·5 **(g)** 42·4 + 39·4 **(h)** 28·8 + 28·1

**3** How many spacewarps did *BETA* travel altogether?

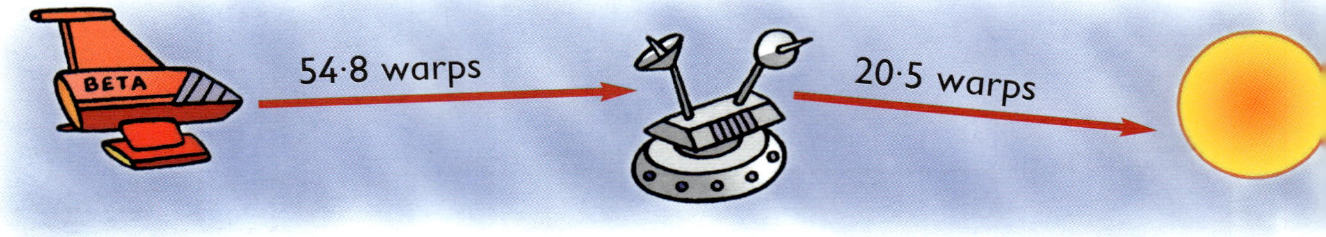


**4** **(a)** 22·8 + 5·5 **(b)** 70·7 + 8·4 **(c)** 4·6 + 33·6 **(d)** 81·1 + 8·9
**(e)** 85·4 + 9·9 **(f)** 7·5 + 67·6 **(g)** 3·7 + 53·7 **(h)** 36·7 + 10·3

**5** On Planet Krypta each weight is **increased by 8·5 kg**.
Find each of these weights **on Krypta.**

**(a)** **(b)** **(c)** **(d)**

**6** **(a)** 7·5 + 8·7 + 14·3 **(b)** 6·4 + 9·9 + 25·6

**1** How much heavier is

**(a)** droid 2 than droid 1
**(b)** droid 4 than droid 3
**(c)** droid 1 than droid 3
**(d)** droid 4 than droid 2
**(e)** droid 4 than droid 1
**(f)** droid 2 than droid 3?

**2** **(a)** 18·2 − 4·9 **(b)** 74·6 − 1·8 **(c)** 38·3 − 3·5 **(d)** 66·1 − 4·4

**(e)** 53·5 − 6·7 **(f)** 87·4 − 8·9 **(g)** 45·7 − 5·8 **(h)** 27·0 − 9·6

**3** How much longer is spaceshuttle *Comet* than spaceshuttle

**(a)** *Laser* **(b)** *Sunburst*
**(d)** *Mercury* **(d)** *Explorer*?

**4** Find the difference between the lengths of

**(a)** *Mercury* and *Explorer*
**(b)** *Sunburst* and *Mercury*
**(c)** *Laser* and *Sunburst*.

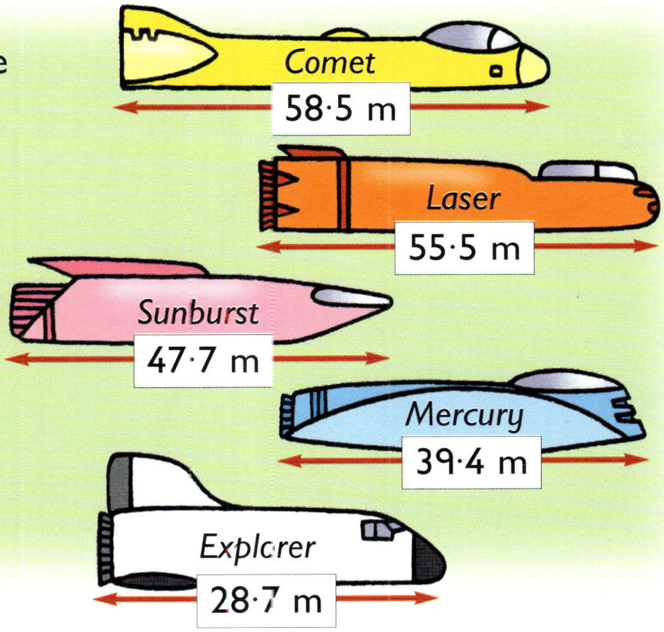


**5** Name each pilot's spaceshuttle.

| Orbit Oil | Meteor Milk | Planet Potion | Jupiter Juice | Saturn Slime |
|---|---|---|---|---|

**1** Find the volume of

**(a)** 2 jars of *Saturn Slime*
**(b)** 8 jars of *Planet Potion*
**(c)** 5 jars of *Meteor Milk*
**(d)** 9 jars of *Jupiter Juice*
**(e)** 4 jars of *Orbit Oil*
**(f)** 7 jars of *Planet Potion*
**(g)** 3 jars of *Meteor Milk*
**(h)** 6 jars of *Saturn Slime*
**(i)** 7 jars of *Jupiter Juice*
**(j)** 9 jars of *Orbit Oil.*

**2** **(a)** 8 × ■ = 7·2 **(b)** ■ × 8 = 4·8 **(c)** 7 × ■ = 3·5 **(d)** ■ × 9 = 6·3

**Spaceflu Cure**
Each capsule contains:
3·2 g of Starsalt
7·8 g of Solarsand
6·4 g of **X**
5·9 g of Moondust

**3** What weight of each ingredient is in

**(a)** 3 capsules **(b)** 7 capsules
**(c)** 9 capsules **(d)** 10 capsules?

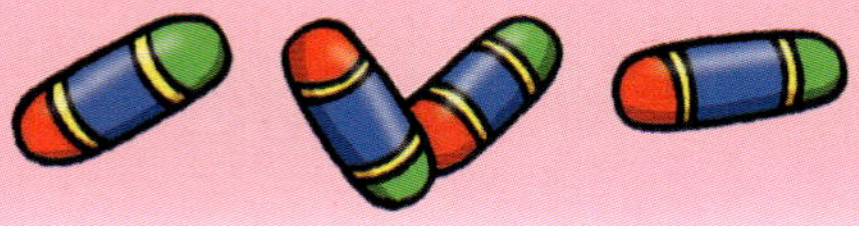

**4** **(a)** 6 × 1·4 **(b)** 2 × 4·5 **(c)** 7 × 2·3 **(d)** 10 × 3·8
**(e)** 9 × 2·6 **(f)** 5 × 7·7 **(g)** 4 × 9·4 **(h)** 3 × 8·9

**5** Doctor Vortex sells Cosmic Cough Mixture in two sizes:

- large bottles - 2·6 ℓ
- small bottles - 1·2 ℓ

She sells 10 litres altogether.

How many of each size does she sell?

**1** Write as a decimal fraction.

**(a)** $\frac{83}{100}$ **(b)** $15\frac{22}{100}$ **(c)** $6\frac{6}{100}$ **(d)** $20\frac{10}{100}$

**(e)** three tenths and six hundredths
**(f)** thirty-three hundredths
**(g)** nine hundredths
**(h)** seven and one hundredth

**2** Copy and complete each sequence.

**(a)** 0·32 — 0·33 — 0·34 — ___ — ___ — ___

**(b)** 0·58 — 0·57 — ___ — 0·55 — ___ — ___

**(c)** 2·44 — 2·46 — ___ — ___ — 2·52 — ___

**(d)** 7·20 — 7·15 — 7·10 — ___ — ___ — ___

**3** Write the number between:

**(a)** 0·75 ___ 0·77
**(b)** 0·10 ___ 0·08
**(c)** 2·25 ___ 2·23
**(d)** 4·98 ___ 5·00

**4** Write **a** number between:

**(a)** 3·53 and 3·58
**(b)** 10·01 and 9·92
**(c)** 4·00 and 4·10
**(d)** 11·22 and 10·01
**(e)** 37·66 and 37·56
**(f)** 100·55 and 99·99

**1** Write the value of the 9 in each number.

(a) 59·65 (b) 38·49 (c) 67·92
(d) 90·03 (e) 25·91 (f) 16·79

**2**

| | | | |
|---|---|---|---|
| 16.75 | 8.44 | 4.84 | 26.51 |
| 25.03 | 33.48 | 54.69 | 19.34 |

Which number has

(a) 3 tenths (b) 5 hundredths (c) 3 tens
(d) the largest hundredths digit (e) the smallest hundredths digit
(f) its tenths digit double its hundredths digit?

**3** Which is the **larger** number?

(a) 6·63 6·36 (b) 4·14 4·21 (c) 8·80 $8\frac{8}{100}$

**4** Which is the **smaller** number?

(a) $\frac{17}{100}$ 0·71 (b) 5·43 5·34 (c) $7\frac{65}{100}$ 7·66

**5** Write in order. Start with the **smallest** number.

(a) 3·46 4·64 6·36 7·01 (b) 2·95 5·92 2·59 9·52
(c) 0·65 0·56 0·06 6·05 (d) 1·10 1·01 10·10 10·01

**6** Write in order. Start with the **largest** number.

(a) 7·37 7·73 3·77 7·03 (b) 5·11 5·01 5·10 5·15
(c) 0·53 0·35 0·05 0·55 (d) 0·90 9·01 1·99 9·19

**7** Round each amount **to the nearest £**.

(a) £6·59 (b) £5·44 (c) £10·08 (d) £19·70

**Ask your teacher for the rules to the games.**

### Decimal Bingo

| | | |
|---|---|---|
| 0·85 | 0·58 | 0·93 |
| 0·55 | 0·81 | 0·73 |

| | | |
|---|---|---|
| 0·73 | 0·90 | 0·42 |
| 0·95 | 0·58 | 0·76 |

| | | |
|---|---|---|
| 0·93 | 0·50 | 0·58 |
| 0·85 | 0·80 | 0·95 |

**1** **(a)** 0·42 + 0·16 = ■ **(b)** 0·14 + 0·28 = ■ **(c)** 0·27 + 0·28 = ■
**(d)** 0·63 + 0·17 = ■ **(e)** 0·17 + 0·56 = ■ **(f)** 0·29 + 0·64 = ■
**(g)** 0·32 + 0·44 = ■ **(h)** 0·12 + 0·38 = ■ **(i)** 0·71 + 0·24 = ■
**(j)** 0·57 + 0·24 = ■ **(k)** 0·34 + 0·56 = ■ **(l)** 0·42 + 0·43 = ■

**2** What colour is the winning card?

### Noughts and Crosses

| | | |
|---|---|---|
| 0·16 | 0·48 | 0·17 |
| 0·44 | 0·50 | 0·30 |
| 0·33 | 0·26 | 0·21 |

**3** Xena plays first. Who wins the game?

| Xena | Oliver |
|---|---|
| **(a)** 0·75 - 0·25 = ■ | **(b)** 0·63 - 0·42 = ■ |
| **(c)** 0·58 - 0·14 = ■ | **(d)** 0·98 - 0·68 = ■ |
| **(e)** 0·32 - 0·15 = ■ | **(f)** 0·72 - 0·39 = ■ |
| **(g)** 0·50 - 0·24 = ■ | **(h)** 0·61 - 0·45 = ■ |
| **(i)** 0·84 - 0·36 = ■ | **(j)** 0·90 - 0·47 = ■ |

### Rows and Columns

**4** Copy and complete so that each row **and** column has a total of 1·0.

**(a)**

| | | |
|---|---|---|
| 0·32 | | 0·40 |
| | 0·63 | 0·16 |
| 0·47 | | |

**(b)**

| | | |
|---|---|---|
| | 0·33 | |
| 0·47 | | 0·43 |
| | 0·57 | |

**Name each winner of Games 1 to 4.**

**Game 1** The player with the highest score wins.

| Sally | John | Mary | Harry |
| --- | --- | --- | --- |
| 8·42 + 1·36 | 5·75 + 4·24 | 7·31 + 2·46 | 6·42 + 3·56 |

**Game 2** The player with lowest score wins.

| Jan | Brad | Lisa | Leo |
| --- | --- | --- | --- |
| 6·47 – 1·31 | 8·64 – 3·52 | 7·87 – 2·26 | 9·85 – 4·43 |

**Game 3** The player with the highest score wins.

| Sanji | Rita | Paulo | Lee - jay |
| --- | --- | --- | --- |
| 4·52 + 1·87 | 4·83 + 2·74 | 2·68 + 3·75 | 3·29 + 3·92 |

**Game 4** The player with the lowest score wins.

| Anja | Barry | Connie | Dale |
| --- | --- | --- | --- |
| 9·39 – 7·72 | 3·81 – 1·39 | 5·60 – 3·94 | 6·12 – 4·69 |

**Give the colour of the winning cards in Games 5 and 6.**

**Game 5** The value of the winning cards is less than 2·69.

| red | yellow | green | blue |
| --- | --- | --- | --- |
| 0·86 + 1·87 | 5·34 – 2·65 | 1·49 + 1·33 | 8·04 – 5·38 |

**Game 6** The value of the winning card is greater than 8·2.

| green | blue | red | yellow |
| --- | --- | --- | --- |
| 4·23 + 3·58 | 10·10 – 2·57 | 9·16 – 0·98 | 3·74 + 4·69 |

# SHOP AT www.things.co.

**1** You have £100 to spend at www.*things.co.*
Make up an order where you spend as close to £100 as possible.
You cannot overspend.

**2** What is the total cost of

**(a)** 18 padlocks **(b)** 13 calculators **(c)** 11 watches?

**3** Jack saved the same amount of money each month for one year.
How much did he save each month to buy the mobile phone?

**4** Zara has saved £19·27 to buy the watch.
How much more does she need to save?

**5** The cost of posting one CD is £3·35.
What is the cost of posting a CD to 27 customers?

**6** What is the cost of two mobile phones in the Special Offer?

www.things.co. www.things.co. www.things.co. www.things.co.

**Special Offer!**

Order two mobile phones and save $\frac{1}{4}$ of the cost.

Each pet blanket sold at *Petcare* has **100 equal parts**.

**1** Find the percentage of each of these blankets

- coloured
- not coloured.

**(a)**

**(b)**

**(c)**

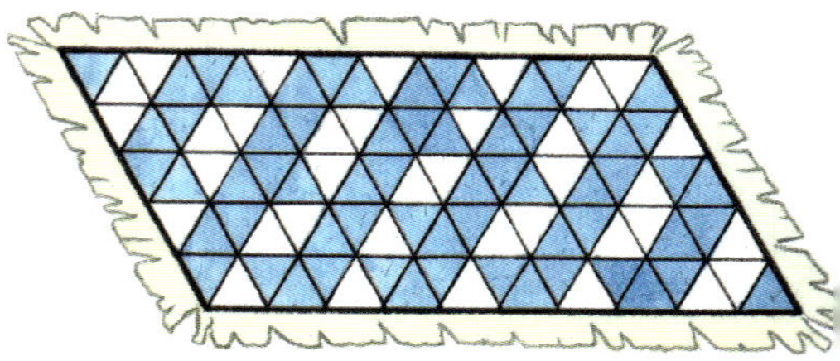

**2** Find the percentage of each blanket

- coloured yellow
- coloured blue
- coloured
- not coloured.

**(a)**

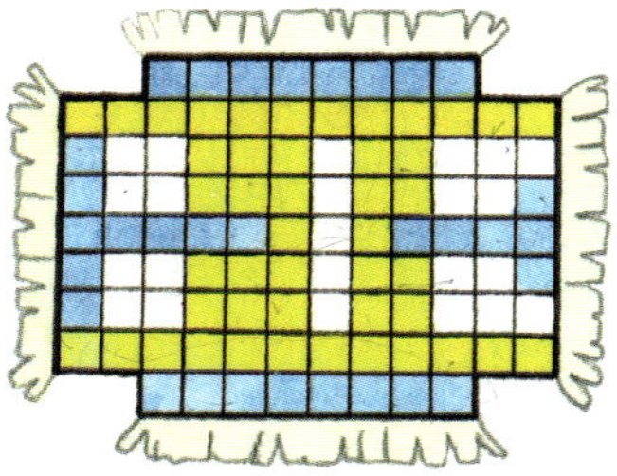

**(b)**

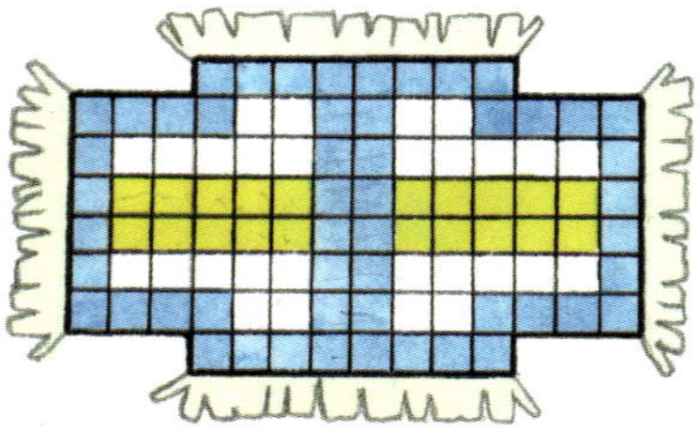

**(c)**

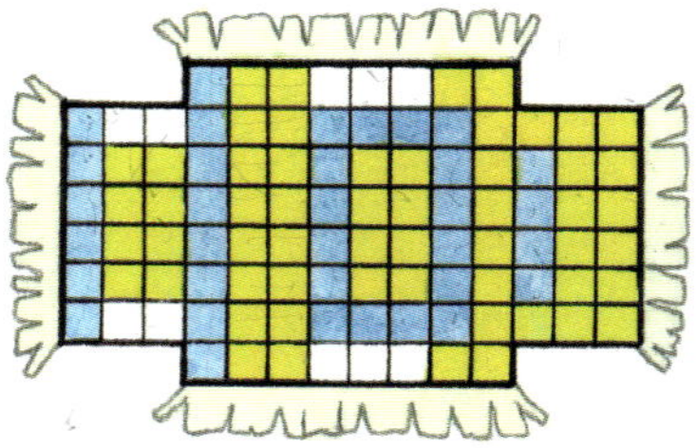

**3** What percentage of this blanket is

**(a)** coloured
**(b)** not coloured
**(c)** neither blue nor geen
**(d)** neither yellow nor blue
**(e)** neither green nor yellow?

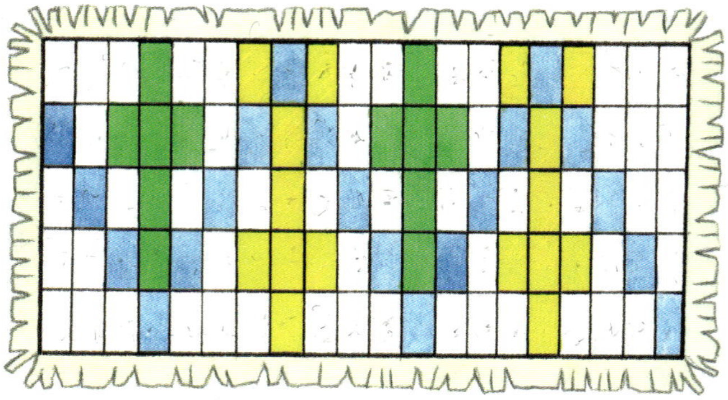

**1** Write as a percentage.

(a) $\frac{17}{100}$ (b) $\frac{53}{100}$ (c) $\frac{6}{100}$ (d) $\frac{60}{100}$

(e) 0·26 (f) 0·95 (g) 0·70 (h) 0·07

**2** Write in **two** other ways.

(a) 16% (b) $\frac{8}{100}$ (c) 0·4 (d) 0·01

(e) $\frac{23}{100}$ (f) 5% (g) 10% (h) 1

**3** Write the percentage of each cat food which is **not** fish.

(a) (b) (c)

**4**

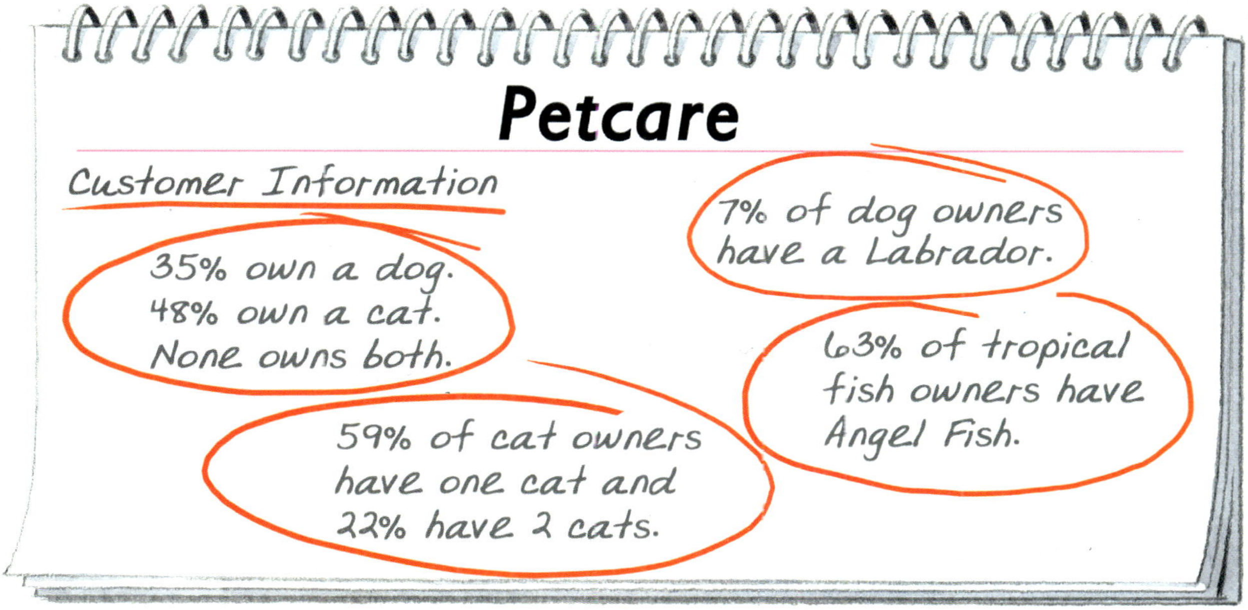


What percentage of

**(a)** tropical fish owners do not have Angel Fish
**(b)** dog owners have breeds other than Labrador
**(c)** cat owners have three or more cats
**(d)** customers own neither a dog nor a cat?

**1** Write the missing numbers in each sequence.

(a) 4, 3, 2, 1, ■, ■, ■, ■
(b) 0, -3, -6, -9, ■, ■, ■, ■
(c) -9, -7, -5, -3, ■, ■, ■, ■
(d) -50, -40, -30, -20, ■, ■, ■, ■
(e) -25, -30, -35, -40, ■, ■, ■, ■
(f) -150, -125, -100, -75, ■, ■, ■, ■

**2** Write

- the lower temperature

(a) -5°C 5°C
(b) -7°C -10°C
(c) 0°C -3°C

- the highest temperature.

(d) -4°C -2°C -6°C
(e) -3°C 0°C -8°C

**3** Write in order.

- Start with the smallest number.

(a) 0, -6, 3
(b) -4, -7, -2, -9
(c) 0, 3, -5, -3, 1

- Start with the largest number.

(d) -20, 5, -15
(e) -60, -25, 10, -2
(f) 10, 6, -7, -10, 4

**4** Write the number between

(a) -18 and -20
(b) -29 and -31
(c) 1 and -1.

**5** Write **a** number between

(a) -4 and 0
(b) -6 and 5
(c) -10 and -15.

**6** Write True (T) or False (F).

(a) -6 > -2
(b) -5 < -7
(c) -3 > 0

**7** Copy and complete to make each number story **true.**

(a) ■ < 0
(b) ■ > -2
(c) -8 < ■ < 1

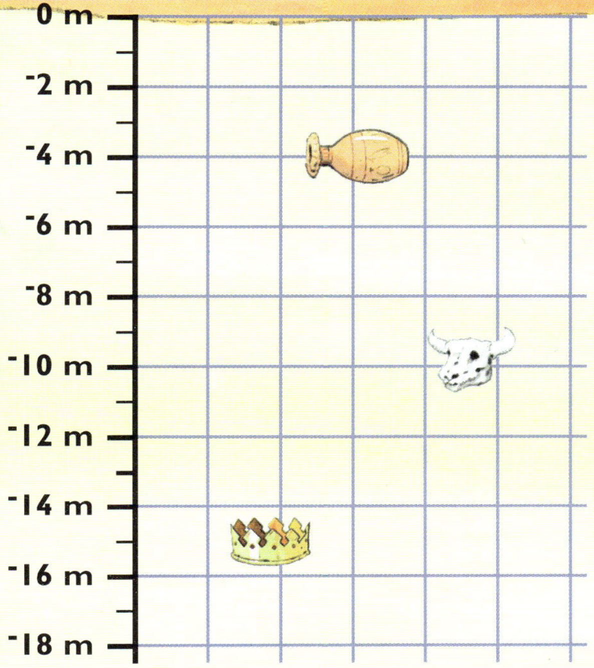


**1** Copy this diagram on squared paper.

**2** Draw

**(a)** a spearhead  at a depth of $^-7$ m

**(b)** a ring  that is 6 m **below** the skull

**(c)** a coin  that is 10 m **above** the crown.

**3** At what depth is a bangle found 5 m **below** the vase?

**4** The top of a stone pillar is 30 m **above** the level of the vase. What is the height of the pillar?

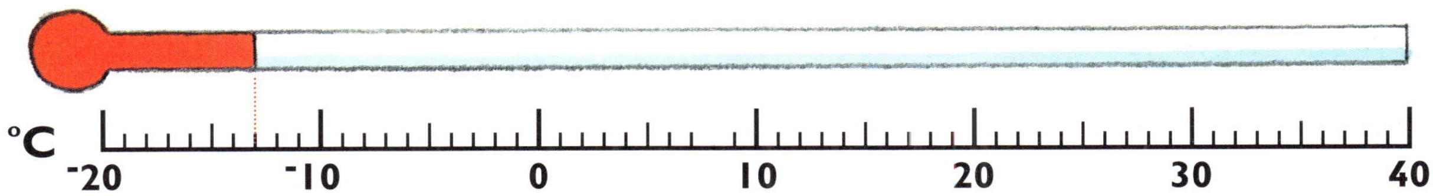


**5** **(a)** What temperature does the thermometer show?
**(b)** What will the temperature be when it rises by 24 degrees?

**6** **(a)** The temperature is 19°C and falls to $^-5$°C. By how many degrees does the temperature fall?
**(b)** The temperature is $^-9$°C. By how many degrees must it rise to reach 11°C?
**(c)** The temperature is $^-4$°C. It falls by 6 degrees and then rises by 10 degrees. What is the temperature now?
**(d)** What is the difference, in degrees, between temperatures of $^-18$°C and 7°C?

**1** Write the **first eight numbers** in each sequence.

**(a)** Start at 45.
Add 23 each time.

**(b)** Start at 200.
Subtract 17 each time.

**(c)** Start at 144.
Increase by 54 each time.

**(d)** Start at 86.
Add 25 each time.

**(e)** Start at 500.
Subtract 19 each time.

**(f)** Start at 849.
Decrease by 21 each time.

**2**
- Write the missing numbers in each sequence.
- Describe the sequence.

**(a)** 210, 226, 242, 258, ■, ■, ■

**(b)** 175, 166, 157, 148, ■, ■, ■

**(c)** 152,182, 212, 242, ■, ■, ■

**(d)** 601, 566, 531, 496, ■, ■, ■

**3**
- Which number is wrong in each sequence?
- What should it be?

**(a)** 34, 48, 62, 86, 90, 104

**(b)** 119, 112, 105, 98, 93, 84

**(c)** 583, 623, 653, 703, 743, 783

**(d)** 547, 516, 485, 454, 423, 394

**4** Start at 57. Add 21 each time.
What is the **tenth** number in the sequence?

**5**

The **sixth** number in my sequence is 175.
I added 25 each time.
What was my starting number?

| | | | | | | | | | | | | | | | | | | | |
|---|---|---|---|---|---|---|---|---|---|---|---|---|---|---|---|---|---|---|---|
| 1 | 2 | 3 | 4 | 5 | 6 | 7 | 8 | 9 | 10 | 11 | 12 | 13 | 14 | 15 | 16 | 17 | 18 | 19 | 20 |
| 21 | 22 | 23 | 24 | 25 | 26 | 27 | 28 | 29 | 30 | 31 | 32 | 33 | 34 | 35 | 36 | 37 | 38 | 39 | 40 |
| 41 | 42 | 43 | 44 | 45 | 46 | 47 | 48 | 49 | 50 | 51 | 52 | 53 | 54 | 55 | 56 | 57 | 58 | 59 | 60 |
| 61 | 62 | 63 | 64 | 65 | 66 | 67 | 68 | 69 | 70 | 71 | 72 | 73 | 74 | 75 | 76 | 77 | 78 | 79 | 80 |
| 81 | 82 | 83 | 84 | 85 | 86 | 87 | 88 | 89 | 90 | 91 | 92 | 93 | 94 | 95 | 96 | 97 | 98 | 99 | 100 |

**1** Write the numbers each child can stand on.

**2** Use your answers to question 1. Which numbers are multiples of

**(a)** 5 and 11 **(b)** 11 and 8 **(c)** 5 and 10 **(d)** 5, 8 and 10?

**3** On which numbers can **both** Ted **and** Saira stand?

**4** Copy the Carroll diagram.
Write these numbers on the diagram.

45 84 66 70 81
21 36 12 54 90

| | Multiple of 6 | ~~Multiple of 6~~ |
|---|---|---|
| Multiple of 9 | | |
| ~~Multiple of 9~~ | | |

**5** Write True (T) or False (F).

**(a)** 111 is a multiple of 11.
**(b)** 102 is a multiple of 8.
**(c)** 117 is a multiple of 9.
**(d)** 700 is a multiple of 10 and 7.
**(e)** 81 is a multiple of 7 and 9.
**(f)** 96 is a multiple of 6 and 8.

**1** **(a)** Which number cards should Leela put in

- the yellow box
- the green box?

**(b)** Explain why some of the number cards should **not** be put in the yellow **or** green boxes.

**2** Write True (T) or False (F).

**(a)** 20 is a factor of 100.

**(b)** 7 has no factors.

**(c)** 12 is not a factor of 50.

**(d)** 23 has only two factors.

**(e)** 15 is a factor of 30 and 50.

**(f)** 8 is a factor of 40 but not a factor of 100.

**3** Copy the Venn diagram. Write the numbers 1 to 20 on the diagram.

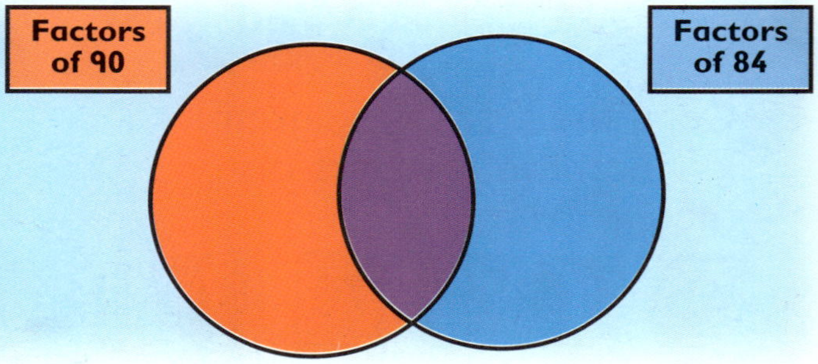


**4** Use **factors** to find

**(a)** $8 \times 13$ **(b)** $6 \times 16$ **(c)** $17 \times 9$

**(d)** $72 \div 6$ **(e)** $126 \div 9$ **(f)** $120 \div 8$

**Measure each length and breadth to the nearest centimetre.**

**1** Find the areas in $cm^2$.

(a)

(b)

(c)

(d)

2 Find the **approximate** areas in $cm^2$.

(a)

(b)

(c)

**3** Draw 2 different rectangles each with an area of 20 $cm^2$.

1 Find the approximate area of each tapestry in square centimetres.

(a)

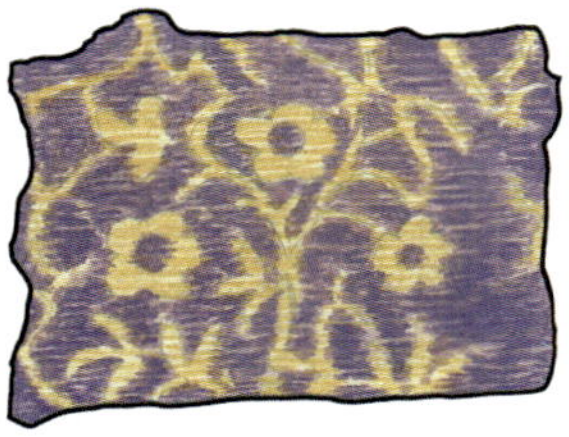

(b)

(c)

(d)

(e)

2 Draw 2 **different** tapestry pieces each with an area of about 24 $cm^2$.

3 Ronan finds a new piece of tapestry.
Its area is about 100 $cm^2$.
The length of the piece is about 4 times the breadth.
What is its approximate length and breadth?

**Work as a group.**
**You need metre sticks, large sheets of paper and sticky tape.**

Megan and Ethan have square Roman mosaic tiles.

1 Make 12 square tiles with sides 50 cm long.

2 (a) Join 4 tiles together to make a larger square like this:

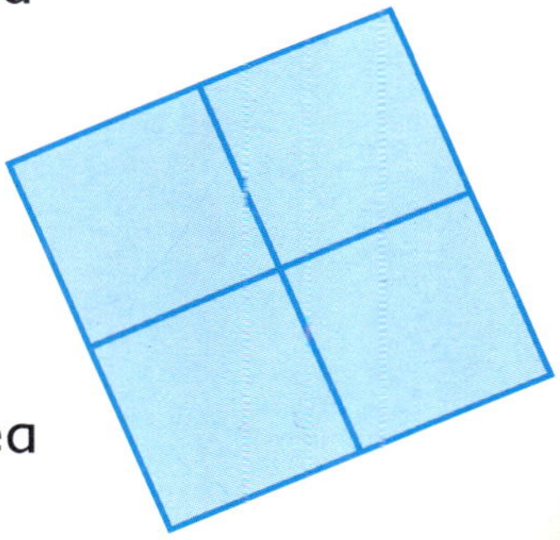

(b) What is the length of each side of the large square?

(c) What is the approximate area of your square?

**The square has an area of about 1 square metre, 1 $m^2$.**

3 (a) Lay 4 tiles together to make each of these shapes.

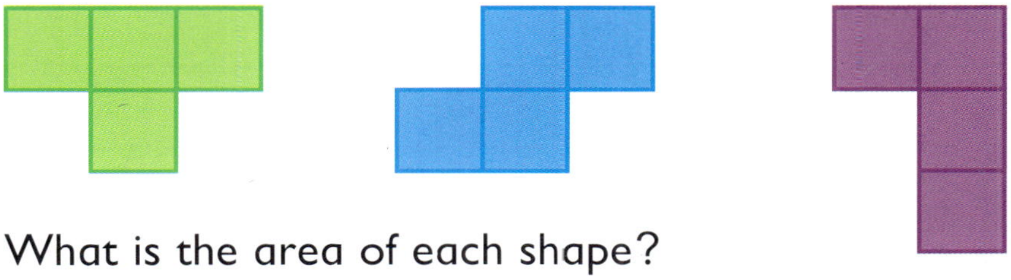

(b) What is the area of each shape?

(c) Make two different shapes each with an area of 2 $m^2$.

**1** Write each time as a 24 – hour time.

(a)

1.15pm

(b)

10.31am

(c)

11.05pm

(d)

9.07pm

(e)

7.51am

(f)

12 noon

**2** Write each time as a 12 – hour time. Use **am** or **pm**.

(a)

17:00

(b)

16:48

(c)

08:45

(d)

19:26

(e)

10:10

(f)

20:11

**3** Find the missing times.

| 12 - hour time | 6.18 pm | (b) | (c) | 12.05 am |
|---|---|---|---|---|
| 24 - hour time | (a) | 09:43 | 14:56 | (d) |

**4** Write these times in order. Start with the earliest.

4.23 pm    10:16    12.01 am    20:38    10.16 pm    04:19

1 Use the events on the notice board to make a programme for tomorrow.
Write all the times as **24-hour** times.

2 Which event takes place

(a) 1st (b) 4th (c) 7th (d) last?

3 Which event starts

(a) 30 minutes after 11.02am (b) 15 minutes before 16:08
(c) 20 minutes after 8.43am (d) 25 minutes before 00:18?

4 Which events take place between

(a) 15:00 and 17:00 (b) 07:00 and 09:00
(c) 11:15 and 15:15 (d) 11:29 and 13:29?

**1** Write the time

**(a)** 25 min after

**(b)** 40 min after

**(c)** 65 min after

**(d)** 80 min after

**(e)** 1h and 15 min after

**(f)** 1h and 50 min after

**(g)** 35 min before

**(h)** 50 min before

**(i)** 75 min before

**(j)** 90 min before

**(k)** 1h and 20 min before

**(l)** 1h and 45 min before

**2** How many minutes are there between each **Start** and **Finish** time?

**(a)** **Start** **Finish**

**(b)** **Start** **Finish**

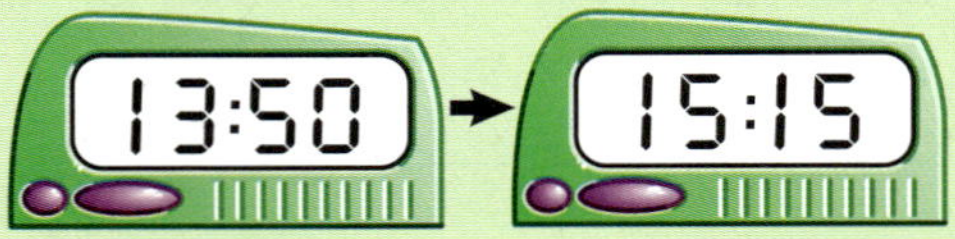


**(c)**

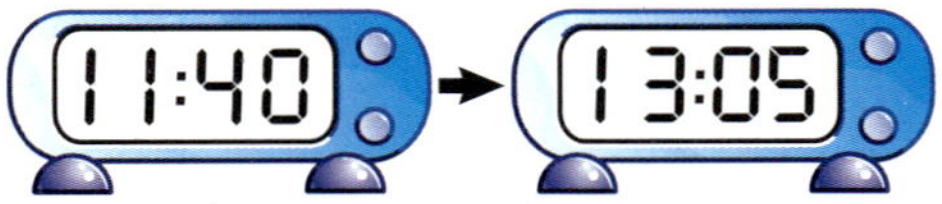


**(d)**

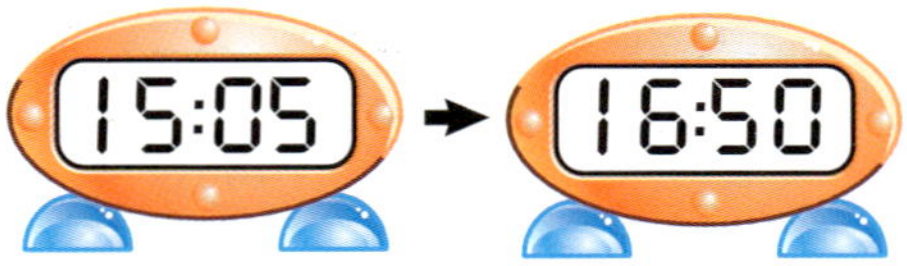


**(e)**

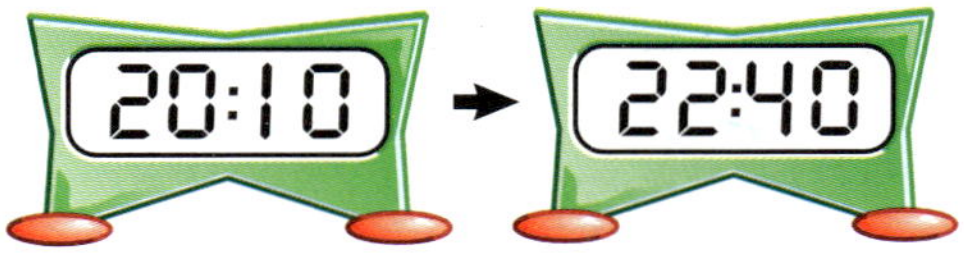


**(f)**

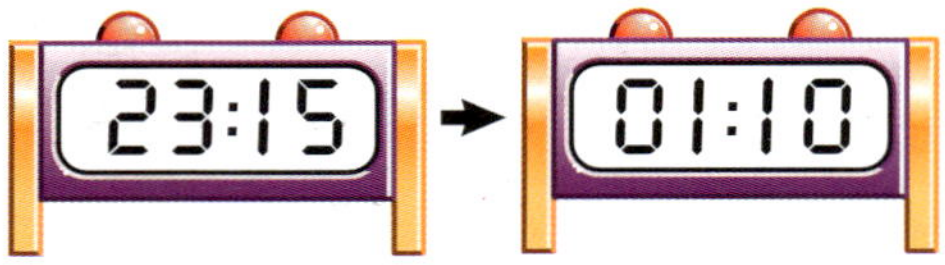

# Speedlink

| | | | | |
|---|---|---|---|---|
| **Bus Station** | 08:05 | 08:55 | 11:15 | 14:30 |
| **City Centre** | 08:20 | 09:20 | 11:25 | 14:40 |
| **Eldon** | 08:40 | 09:45 | 11:40 | 15:55 |
| **Lanbow** | 09:20 | 10:20 | 12:15 | 16:25 |
| **Walston** | 09:50 | 10:45 | 12:35 | 16:50 |
| **Ashford** | 10:15 | 11:10 | 12:55 | 17:15 |

**1** How long does it take

**(a)** the 08:05 bus to reach the City Centre
**(b)** the 08:55 bus to reach Eldon
**(c)** the 11:15 bus to reach Walston?

**2** How long is the journey time between

**(a)** Lanbow and Ashford on the 11:15 bus
**(b)** City Centre and Walston on the 14:30 bus?

**3** The 11:15 bus is 20 minutes late leaving Eldon.
At what time does it arrive in Ashford?

**4** Lisa boards the 08:05 bus at City Centre.
She gets off 90 minutes later.
**Where** does she get off the bus?

**5** Sunil got off the bus at Ashford at 11:10.
His journey had taken 110 minutes.
Where did he board the bus?

**6** An overnight Speedlink coach left the Bus Station at 19:30.
It arrived in Croxford at 06:30.
How long did the journey take?

**1** Estimate then measure each length:

**(a)** the width of a window
**(b)** the width of the teacher's desk
**(c)** the height of the teacher
**(d)** the height of your chair
**(e)** the length of a gym rope
**(f)** the length of a gym bench.

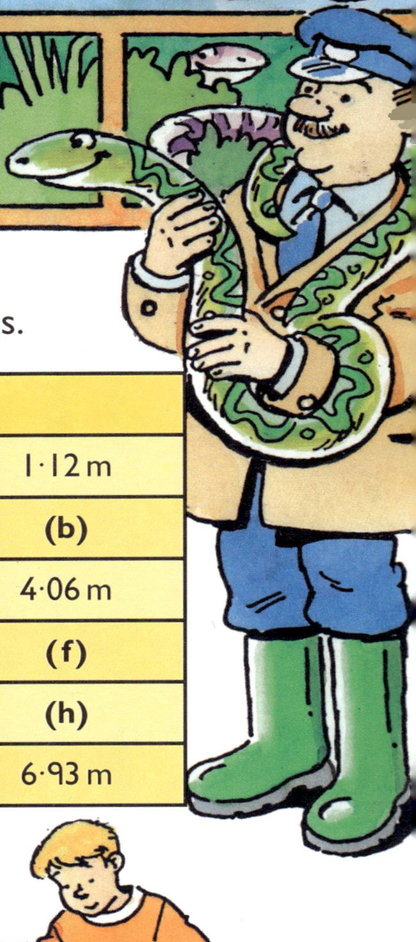

**2** Write the length of each snake in two **other** ways.

| **Snake** | **Length of Snake** | | |
|---|---|---|---|
| Adder | 1 m 12 cm | 112 cm | 1·12 m |
| Boa | 2 m 34 cm | **(a)** | **(b)** |
| Anaconda | **(c)** | **(d)** | 4·06 m |
| Cobra | **(e)** | 328 cm | **(f)** |
| Viper | 2 m 61 cm | **(g)** | **(h)** |
| Python | **(i)** | **(j)** | 6·93 m |

**3** Use chalk to draw a snake

**(a)** 1·25 m long
**(b)** 2·38 m long.

**1** What fraction of a metre is each coloured part of Ahmed's stick?

**2** Use a metre stick or a tape marked in tenths of a metre.
Measure objects like these to the **nearest tenth of a metre**.

**3** Alan jumped $\mathbf{2\frac{7}{10}}$ **m** or **2·7 m.**

Write the length of each of these jumps in another way.

| | **Jade** | **David** | **Anna** | **Li** | **Stuart** |
|---|---|---|---|---|---|
| **Length of jump** | $2\frac{4}{10}$ m | **(b)** | $3\frac{1}{10}$ m | **(d)** | $4\frac{5}{10}$ m |
| | **(a)** | 3·6 m | **(c)** | 2·9 m | **(e)** |

**4** Measure the length of your own jump to the nearest tenth of a metre.

**5** Write in order.

**(a)** Start with the shortest.

| | | | | |
|---|---|---|---|---|
| 123 cm | 1 m 28 cm | 1·2 m | $1\frac{1}{4}$ m | $1\frac{3}{10}$ m |

**(b)** Start with the longest.

| | | | | |
|---|---|---|---|---|
| $3\frac{3}{4}$ m | 3·8 m | 372 cm | $3\frac{1}{2}$ m | $3\frac{7}{10}$ m |

**1** What is the length of the yellow brick in **millimetres**?

**2** Measure each length. Write it in centimetres **and** in millimetres.

**(a)**
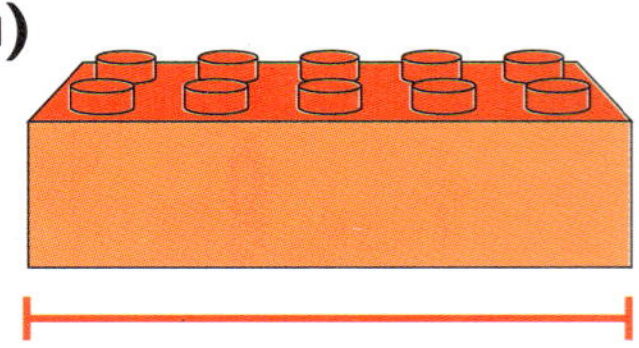

**(b)**
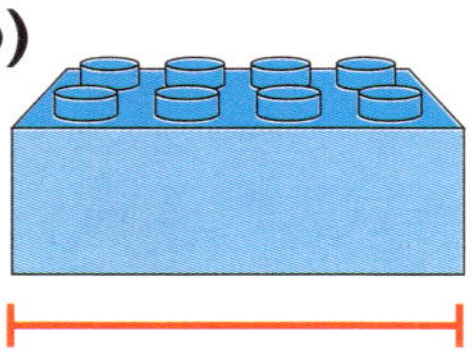

**(c)**
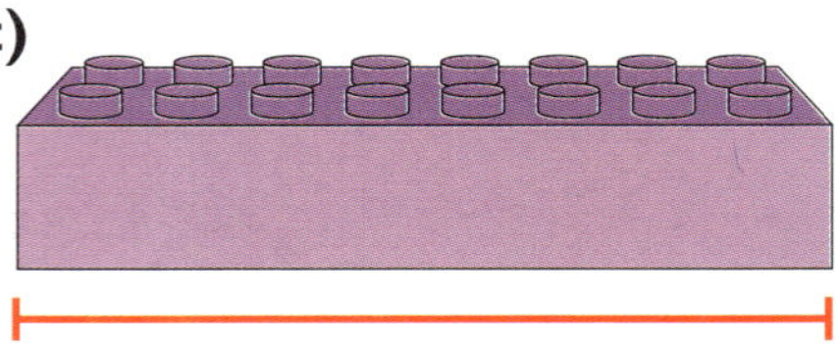

**(d)**
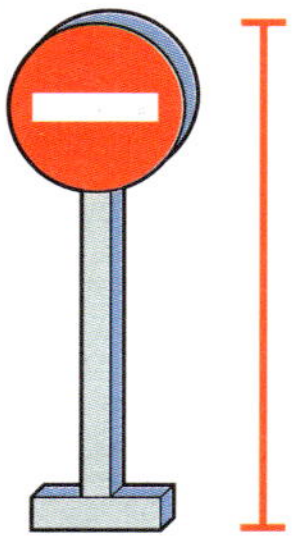

**(e)**

**(f)**

**3** Write in millimetres.

**(a)** 7cm **(b)** $10\frac{1}{2}$ cm **(c)** 15cm **(d)** $16\frac{1}{2}$ cm **(e)** $20\frac{1}{2}$ cm

**4** Write in centimetres.

**(a)** 90 mm **(b)** 65 mm **(c)** 120 mm **(d)** 145 mm **(e)** 305mm

**5** Find the distance between the arrows in cm **and** in mm.

**(a)**
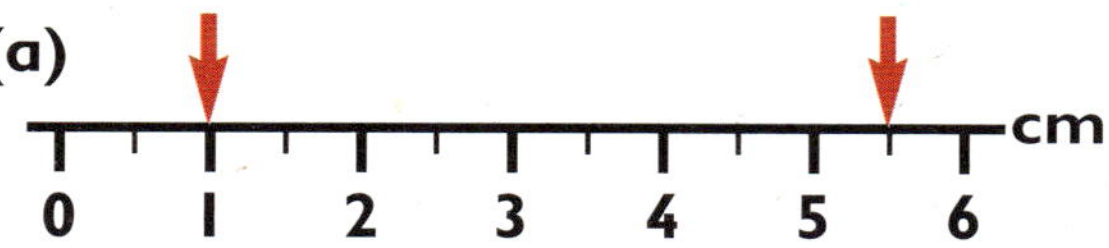


**(b)**
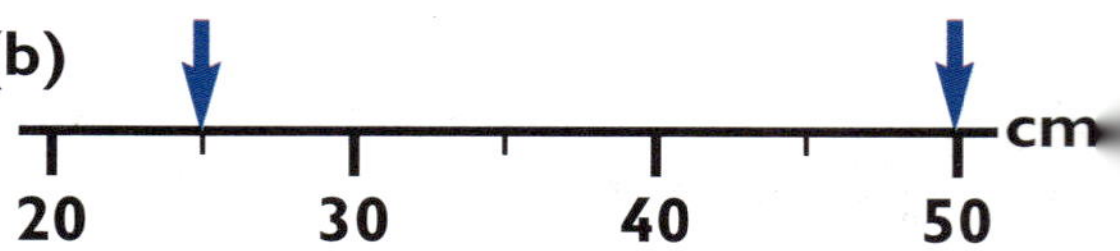

**1** **(a)** Mark out a square of side 25 metres.

**(b)** Find how long you take to walk around its perimeter.

**(c)** Estimate how long you would take to walk **1 kilometre.**

**2** Write in metres.

| | | | |
|---|---|---|---|
| **(a)** 2 km | **(b)** 5 km | **(c)** $3\frac{1}{2}$ km | **(d)** $\frac{3}{10}$ km |
| **(e)** 4 km 300 m | **(f)** $2\frac{1}{10}$ km | **(g)** 3 km 230 m | **(h)** $1\frac{1}{4}$ km |
| **(i)** $1\frac{8}{10}$ km | **(j)** 1 km 507 m | **(k)** $\frac{9}{10}$ km | **(l)** 5 km 342 m |

**3** Write in kilometres and metres.

| | | | |
|---|---|---|---|
| **(a)** 2168 m | **(b)** 1820 m | **(c)** 3004 m | **(d)** 7060 m |

**4** Write in kilometres.

| | | | |
|---|---|---|---|
| **(a)** 7000 m | **(b)** 5000 m | **(c)** 2500 m | **(d)** 8700 m |

**5**

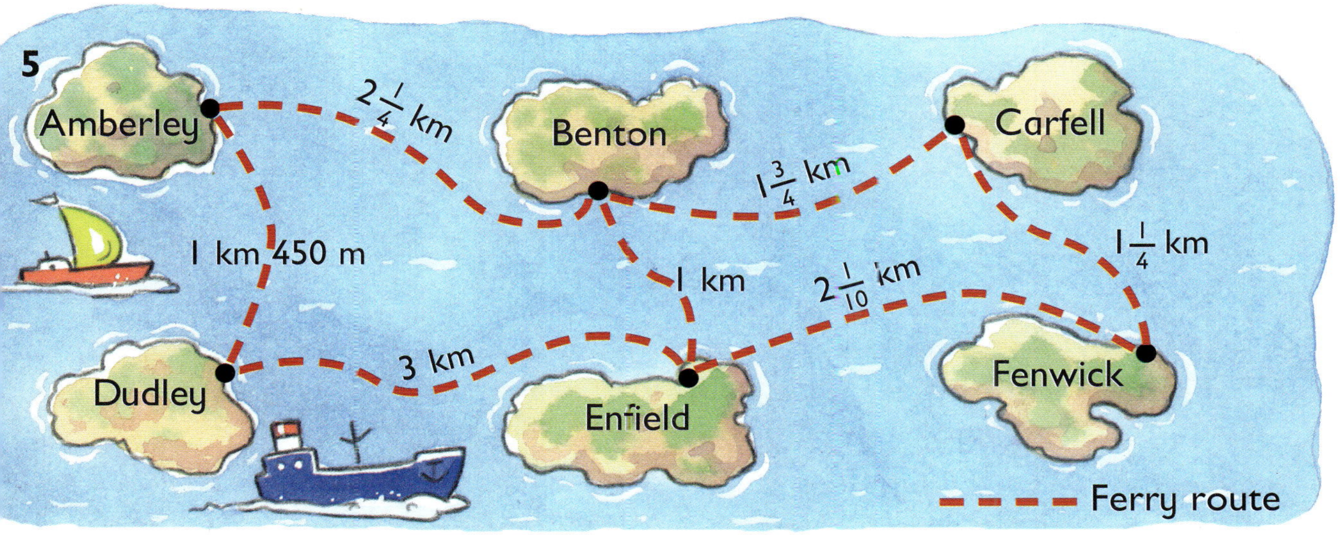


Write in metres the **shortest** distance between

**(a)** Amberley and Enfield

**(b)** Benton and Fenwick

**(c)** Dudley and Carfell

**(d)** Amberley and Fenwick.

**1** Which of these units of length would be best to use for each measurement?

| millimetres | centimetres | metres | kilometres |
|---|---|---|---|

**(a)**

length of your shoe

**(b)**

length of a lorry

**(c)**

distance around your head

**(d)**

height of a tree

**(e)**

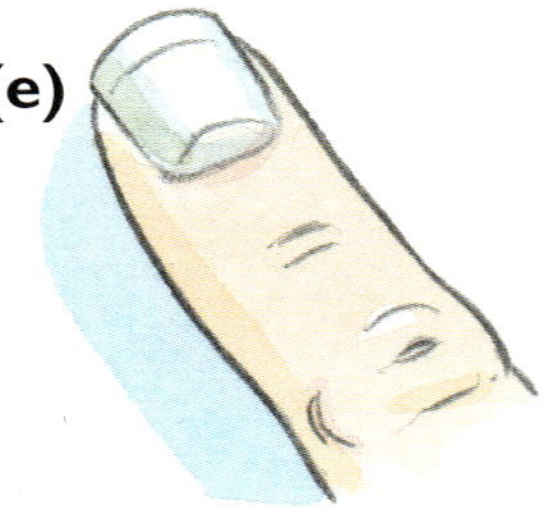

length of your fingernail

**(f)**

distance between Paris and London

**2** Write another item you would measure in

**(a)** metres **(b)** millimetres **(c)** kilometres **(d)** centimetres.

**3**

Each book is 17 mm thick.
Would a set of 30 of these books fit on a shelf 50 cm long?
Explain.

**4** Mary walked 2 kilometres.
David walked 300 m less than Mary.
Tina walked 750 m more than David.
Find the distance walked by **(a)** David **(b)** Tina.

**5** Ben's rope is 4 metres longer than Sue's.
Their ropes have a total length of 20 m.

How long is **(a)** Ben's rope **(b)** Sue's rope?

1 **Calculate** the perimeter of each shape.

(a)

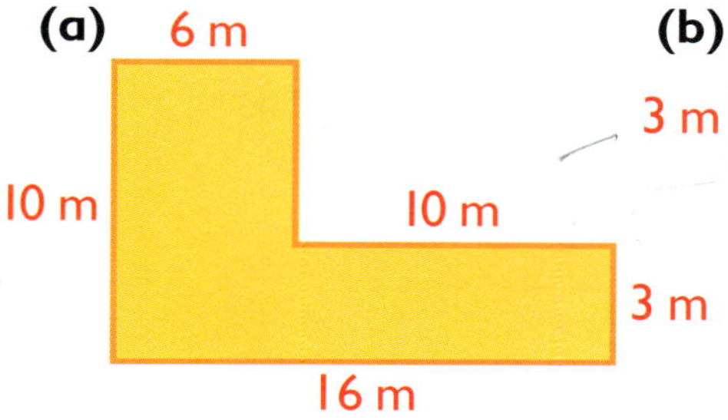


(b)

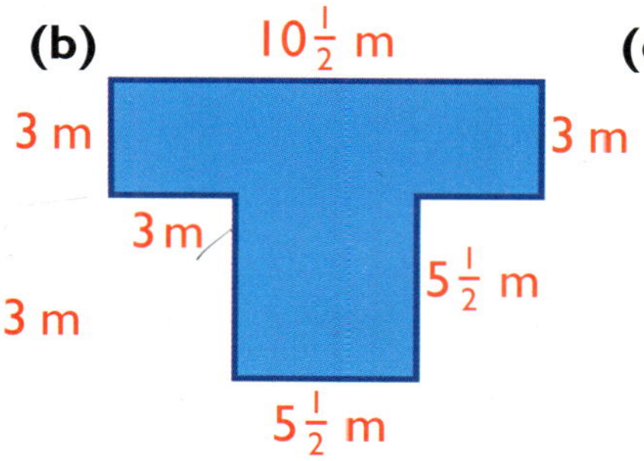


(c)

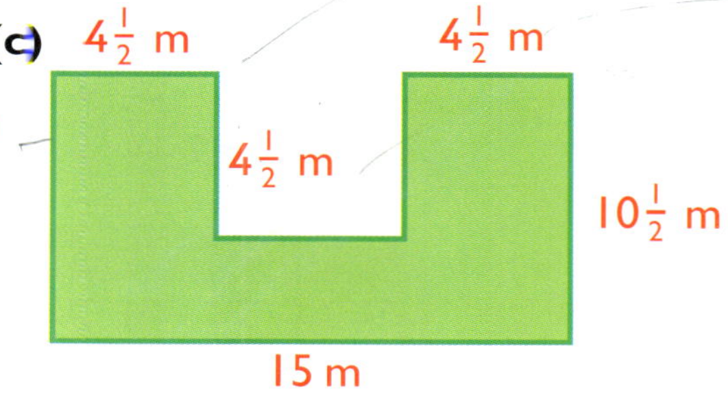


2 (a) **Measure** the length and breadth of each rectangle in centimetres. Copy and complete the table

| Rectangle | Length | Breadth | Perimeter |
|---|---|---|---|
| A | | | |
| B | | | |
| C | | | |

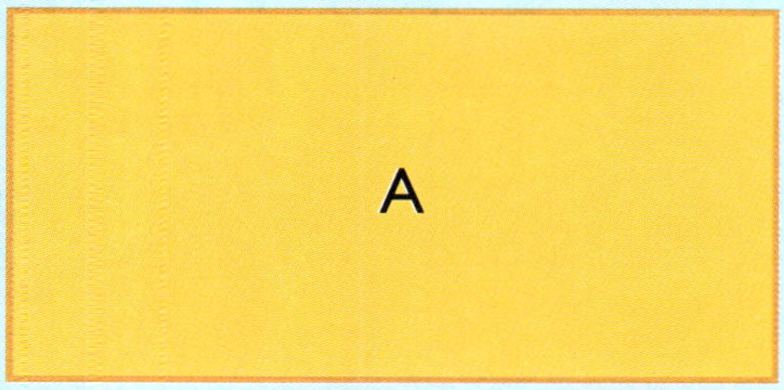


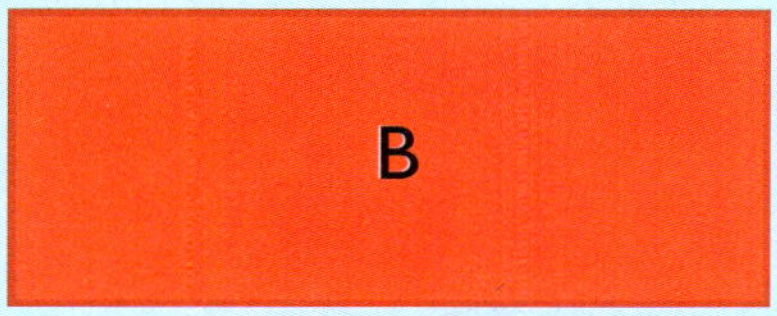

(b) How can you calculate the perimeter of a rectangle when you know its length and breadth?

3 (a) Measure the perimeter of each **regular** polygon in centimetres.

(b) How can you find the perimeter of a **regular** polygon?

4 **Calculate** the side length of this regular octagon.

**1** Write the weight of each item **to the nearest 100 g.**

| onions | carrots | potatoes | turnips |
|---|---|---|---|
| 108g | 384g | 750g | 2040g |

**2** Find the approximate weight of each bag.

**3** Make up bags with these weights.

- **F** about 600g
- **G** about 400g
- **H** about 250g

**4** Find an object which weighs

**(a)** less than 100g
**(b)** between 650g and 850g
**(c)** about 1kg 200g.

**1** Write in grams.

**(a)** $2\frac{3}{4}$ kg **(b)** $1\frac{7}{10}$ kg **(c)** $3\frac{3}{10}$ kg **(d)** $4\frac{1}{10}$ kg

**(e)** 1 kg 210 g **(f)** 3 kg 250 g **(g)** 1 kg 75 g **(h)** 2 kg 200 g

**2** Write in kilograms and grams.

**(a)** $3\frac{1}{2}$ kg **(b)** $2\frac{1}{4}$ kg **(c)** $6\frac{6}{10}$ kg **(d)** $5\frac{4}{10}$ kg

**(e)** 3510 g **(f)** 2050 g **(g)** 1718 g **(h)** 4605 g

**3** Write the weights in order.

**(a)** Start with the heaviest.

**(b)** Start with the lightest.

**4** Write each new weight in kg and g.

**(a)** Add 400 g.

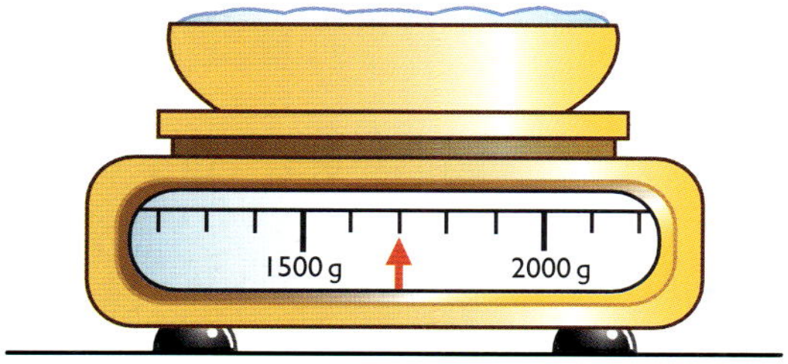


**(b)** Remove 300 g.

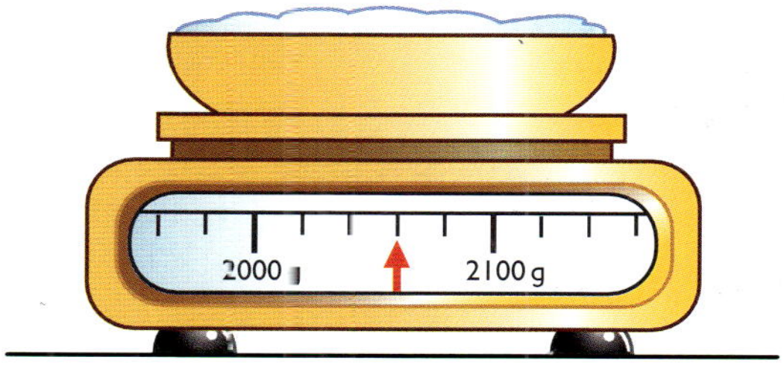


**(c)** Double the weight.

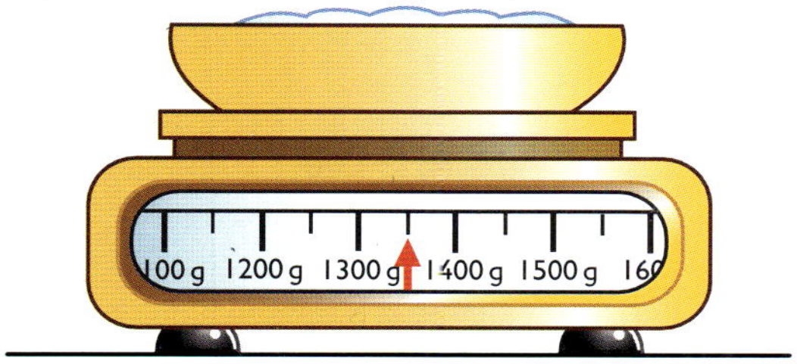


**(d)** Halve the weight.

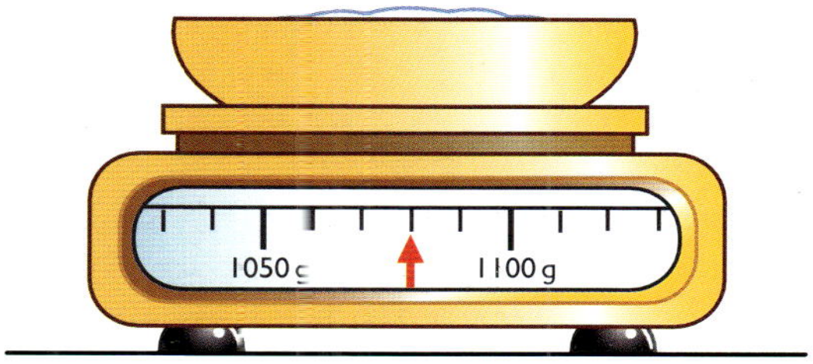

**1** Write each amount in millilitres.

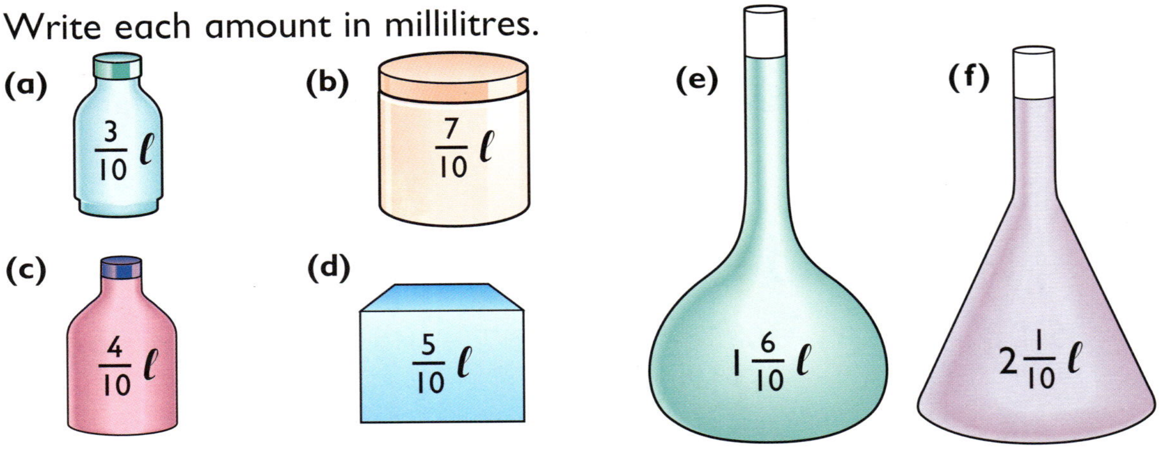


**2** Write in order.

**(a)** Start with the smallest volume.

**(b)** Start with the largest volume.

**3** How many millilitres of cream altogether are on each tray?

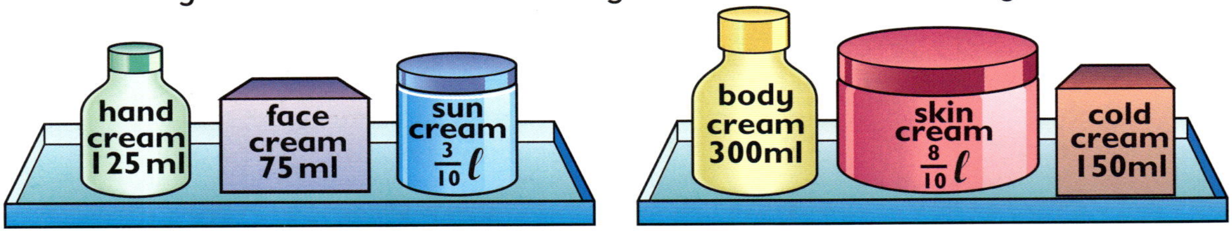


**4** Which two containers together hold

**(a)** $\frac{1}{2}$ litre **(b)** 1 litre

**(c)** $1\frac{1}{2}$ litre **(d)** $\frac{1}{4}$ litre?

**5** Which **three** containers together hold

**(a)** 1 litre **(b)** 2 litres?

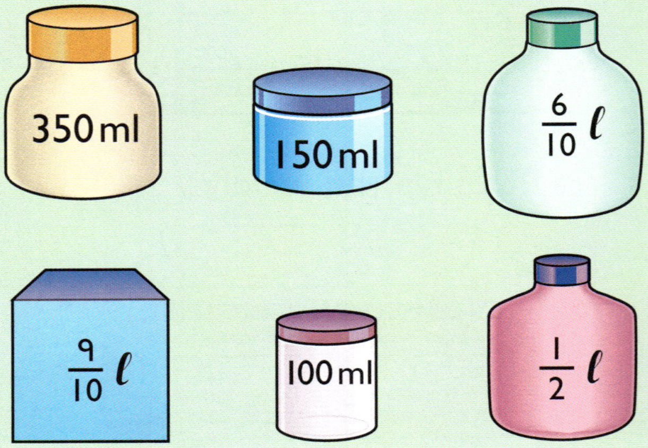

**You need containers like these, a 1 litre measuring jar and a funnel.**

1 **(a)** Estimate the capacity of each container and check by measuring.

Record your results in a table like this.

| Container | Estimate | Measurement |
|---|---|---|
| A | about | about |
| B | | |
| C | | |

**(b)** List the containers in order, starting with the greatest capacity.

2 Find the weight of

**(a)** 1 litre of water **(b)** $\frac{1}{2}$ litre of water.

**1** List the items whose capacities Sally should measure in

**(a)** millilitres **(b)** litres.

**2** Write two other items whose capacities should be measured in

**(a)** millilitres **(b)** litres.

**3**

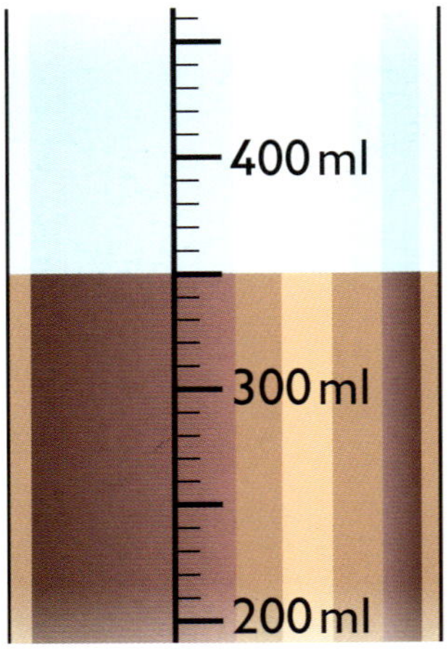


What should be the reading on the scale if Sally **added** the contents of the

**(a)** red bowl **(b)** blue bowl
**(c)** green bowl **(d)** yellow bowl
**(e)** red **and** green bowls
**(f)** yellow **and** green bowls?

**4** How much liquid should Sally pour from the jug into the tub so that both have the same amount?

**5**

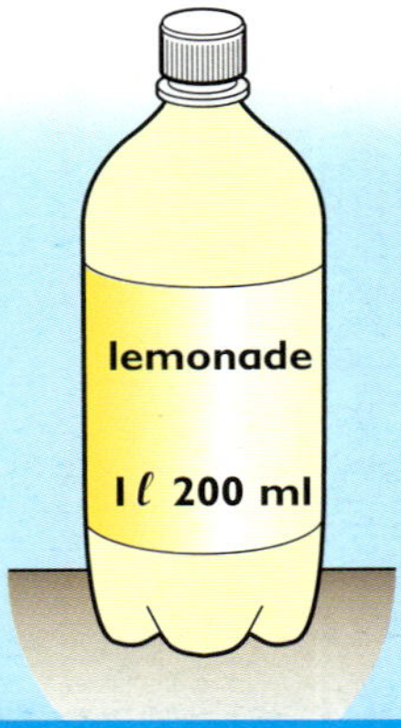


Sally empties the lemonade into a jug and a glass.
She pours 3 times as much into the jug as into the glass.

What volume of lemonade is in the **(a)** jug **(b)** glass?

**Use centimetre cubes.**

1 **(a)** Make these pieces from the puzzle.
Find the volume of each in cubic centimetres.

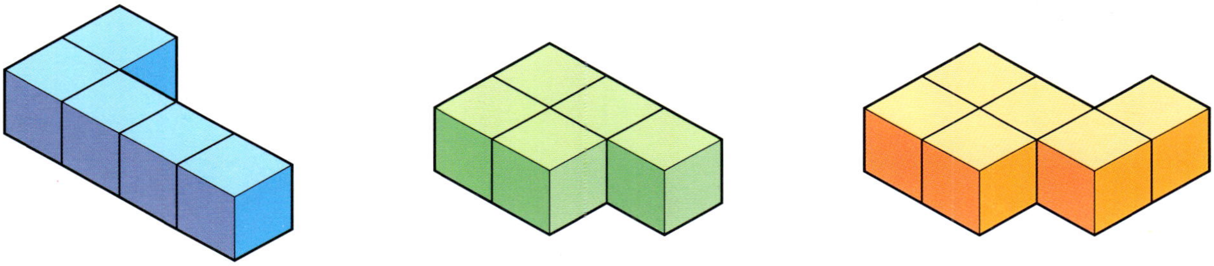

**(b)** Put the three pieces together to make a cuboid and find its volume.

2 Repeat question **1** for these pieces.

3 Find the volume in $cm^3$ of each of these pieces.

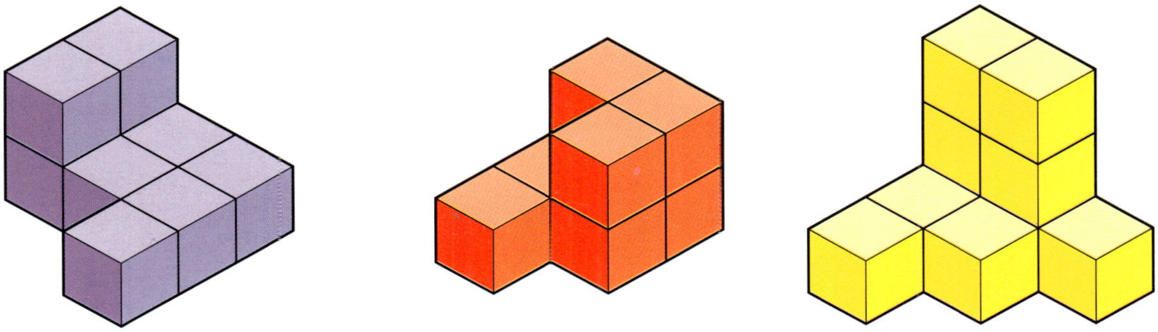

**Use centimetre cubes.**

**1** For each shape find

**(a)** the volume in cubic centimetres
**(b)** the least number of cubes needed to make it a cuboid
**(c)** the volume of the **cuboid**.

**2** Check by building each cuboid.

**(a)**

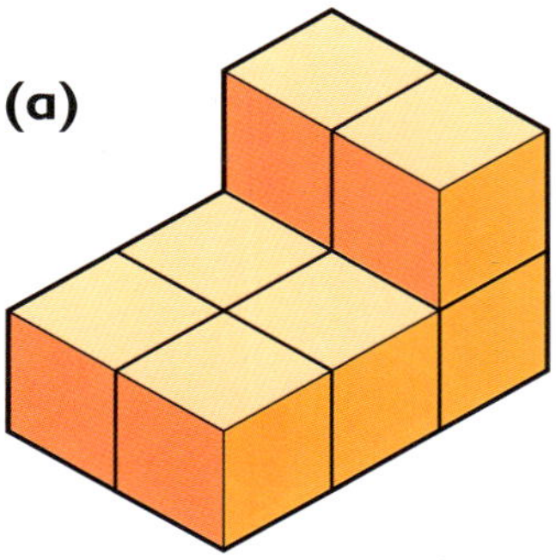

**(b)**

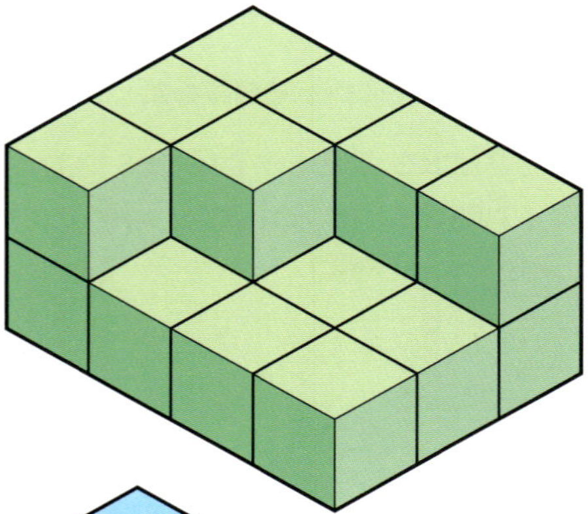

**(c)**

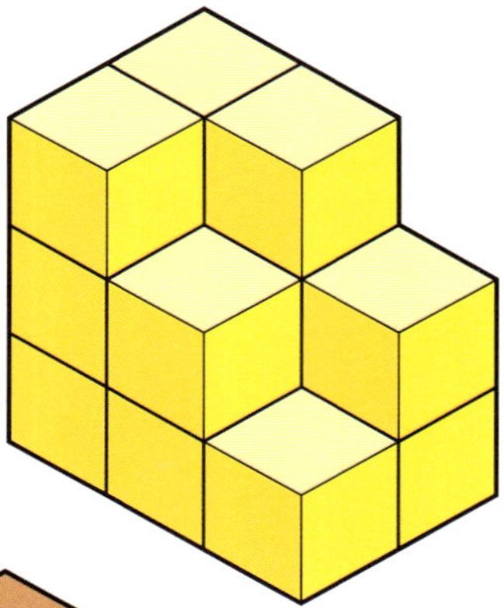

**(d)**

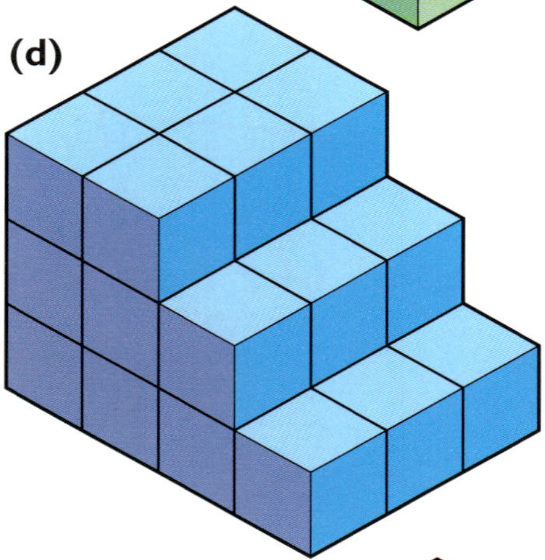

**(e)**

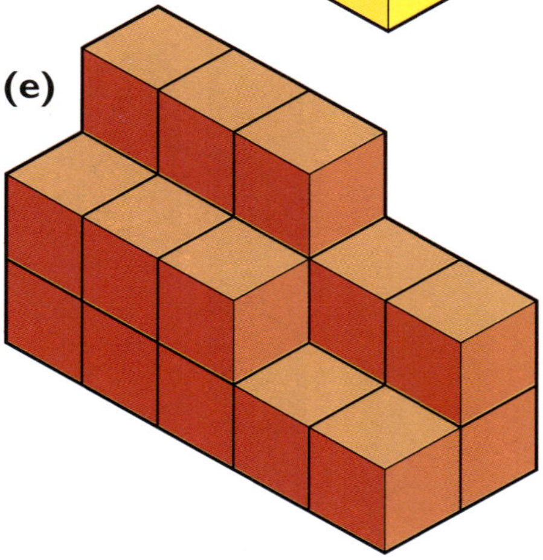

**(f)**

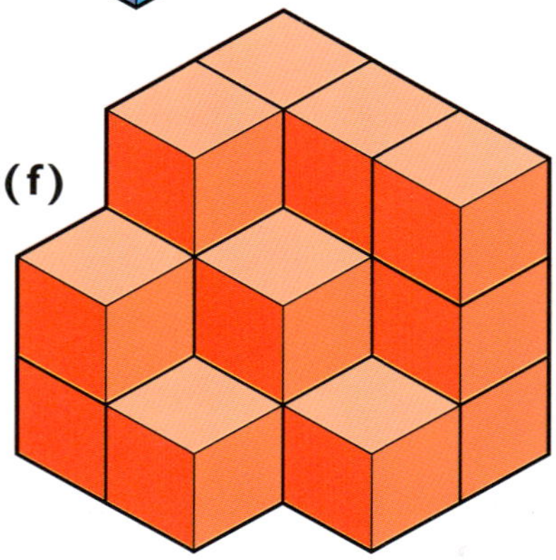

**3** Make as many different cuboids as you can, each with a volume of 20 $cm^3$.

**1** About how many **kilometres** is the distance to

**(a)** Melchester **(b)** Dirleton **(c)** Penby?

**2**

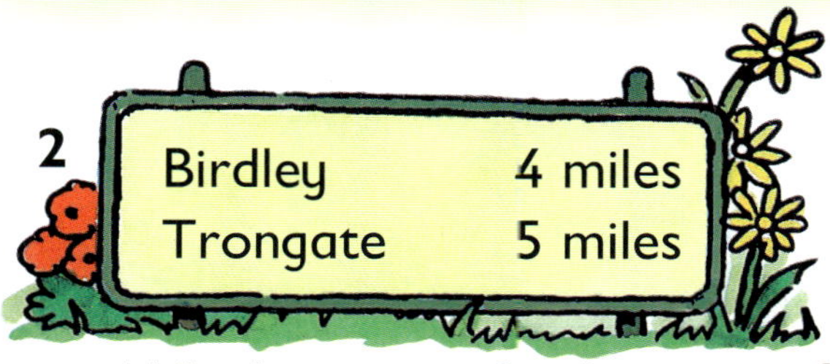


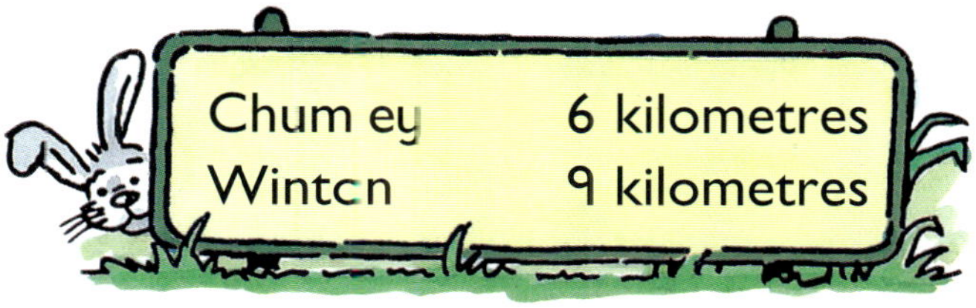


Which town is further away?

**(a)** Birdley or Chumley **(b)** Trongate or Winton?

**3** About how many millilitres are there in

**(a)** 2 pints **(b)** 5 pints?

**4** Which is the greater volume, 3 pints of milk or $1\frac{3}{4}$ litres of milk?

**5**

Which vehicle's fuel tank has the smaller capacity?

tank holds 8 gallons

tank holds 42 litres

**1** **(a)** This jug has 365 ml of milk in it. How much will be left after I pour out 180 ml?

**(b)** This rope is 5 metres long. What length is left when I cut off 65cm?

**(c)** My dog weighs 18 kilograms. My brother is two and a half times as heavy. What is his weight?

**(d)** The capacity of the bucket is 5 litres. The cup holds one quarter of a litre. How many cupfuls of water are needed to fill the bucket?

**2** Sarah needs four lemons to make 400 ml of lemonade. What volume of lemonade can she make with twelve lemons?

**3** List the ingredients for 24 of these cakes.

**Ingredients for 6 cakes**

| | |
|---|---|
| 100g | flour |
| 80g | butter |
| 50g | sugar |
| 2 | eggs |

**4**

How many pieces of string, each 40 cm long, can be cut from a 3 m length?

**5** Sandra buys 20 litres of orange juice for a party. How many **glasses** of orange can she pour if each glass holds 200 millilitres?

**1** Which diagrams show **parallel** lines?

**(a)**

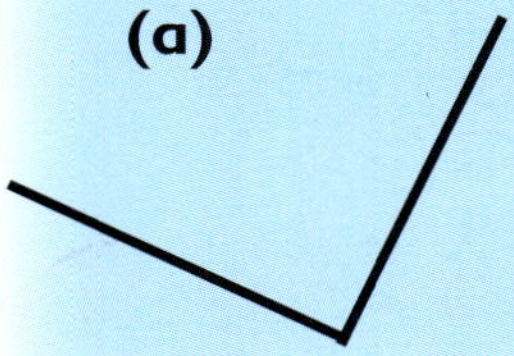

**(b)**

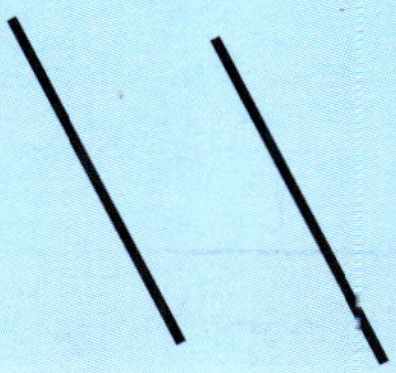

**(c)**

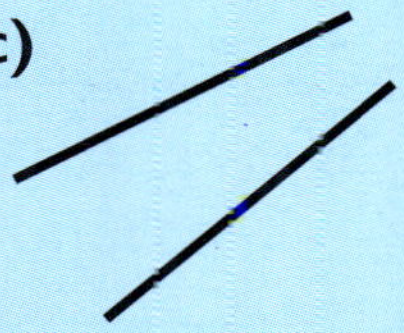

**(d)**

**2** Which diagrams show **perpendicular** lines?

**(a)**

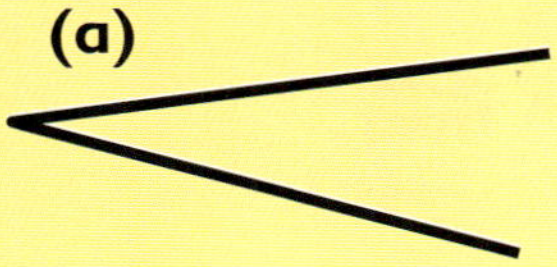

**(b)**

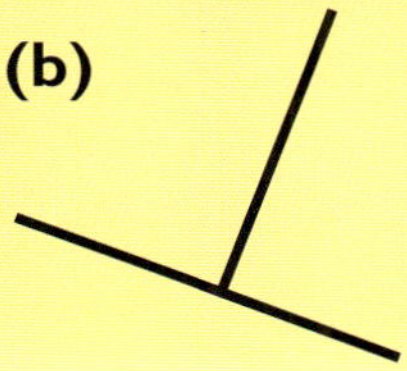

**(c)**

**(d)**

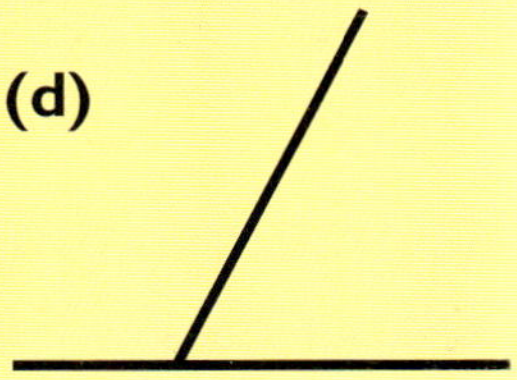

**3** Which shapes have

**(a)** parallel lines and **no** perpendicular lines
**(b)** perpendicular lines and no parallel lines
**(c)** parallel lines **and** perpendicular lines
**(d)** neither parallel lines nor perpendicular lines?

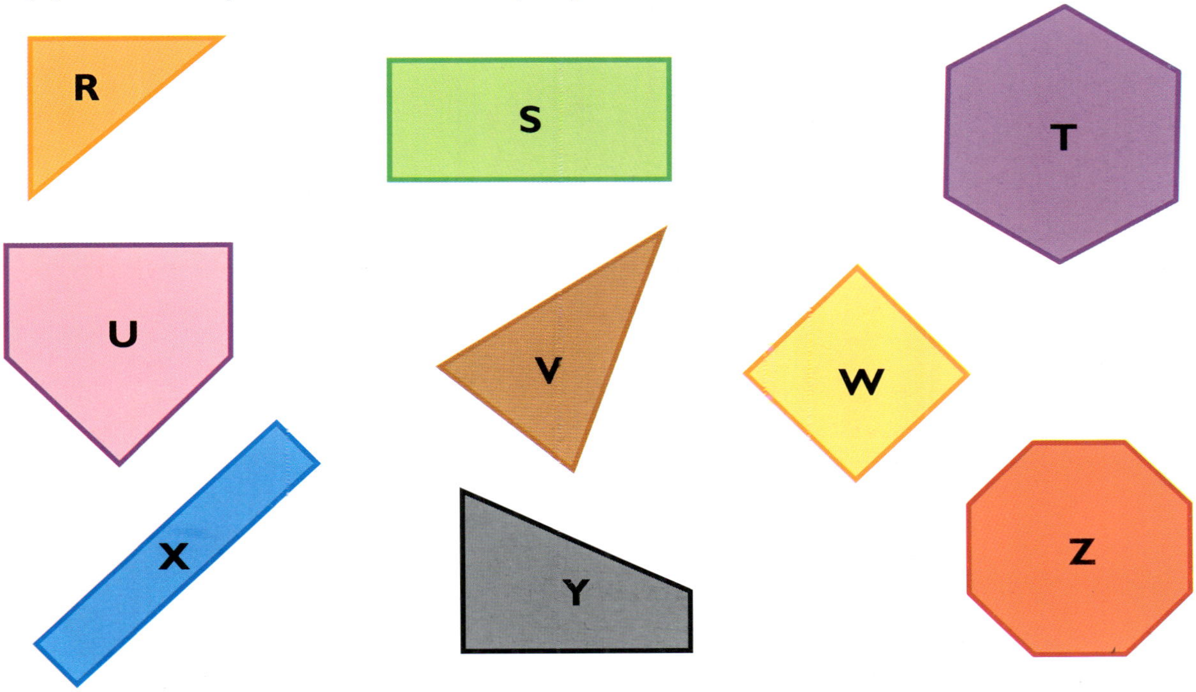

**1** Which of the shapes is Zoë describing?

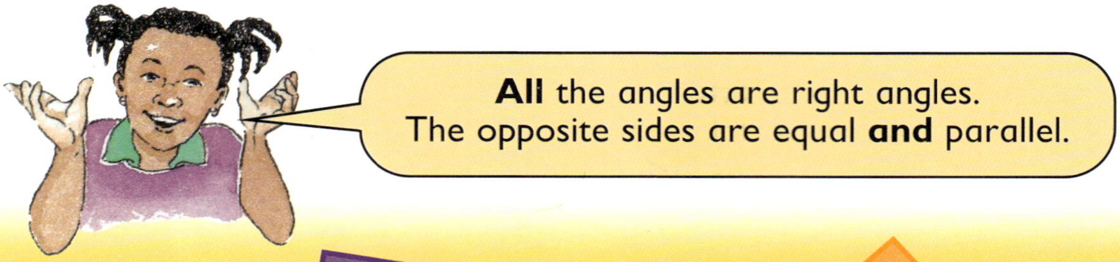

**2** Name the shapes
**(a)** with more than two diagonals
**(b)** with **only** two right angles
**(c)** with opposite sides that are equal **and** parallel
**(d)** that are irregular.

**1** Which triangles could each child be describing?

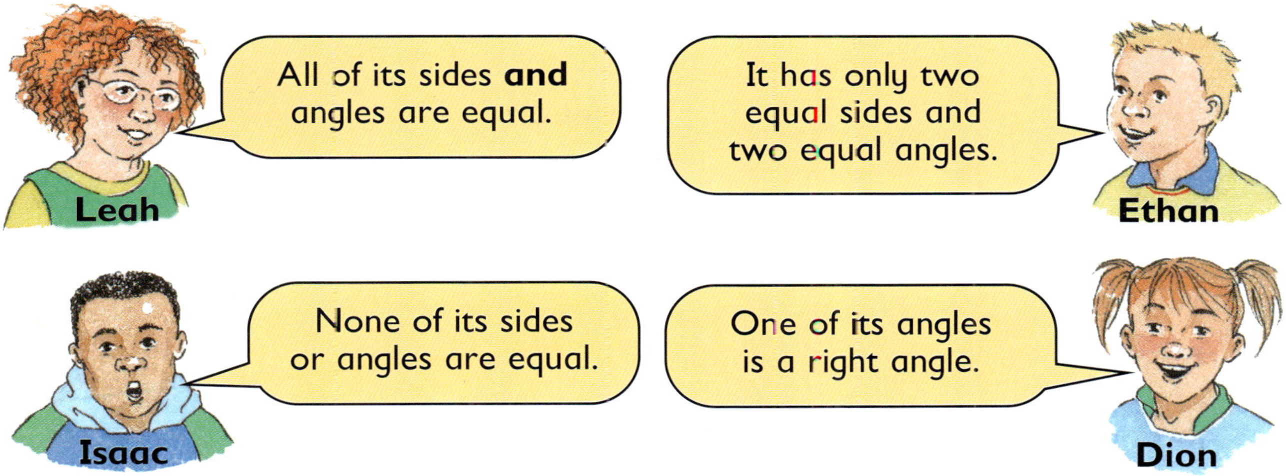

**2** Draw another triangle which matches each description.

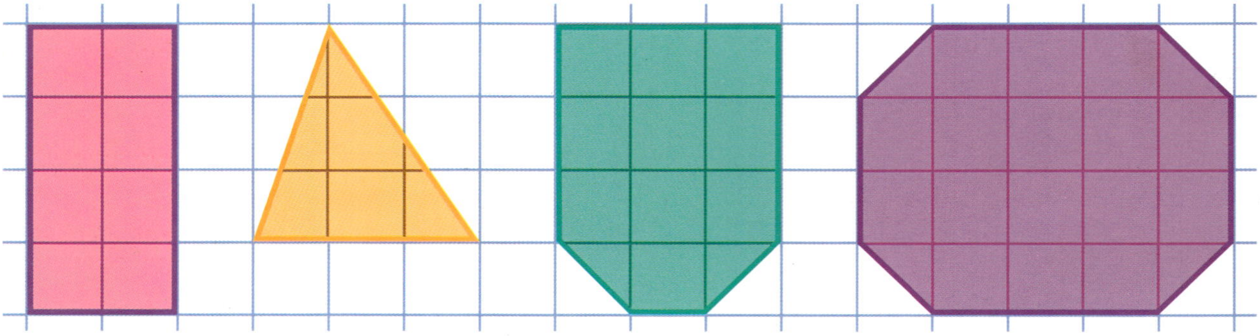

1 (a) Copy each shape on squared paper.
(b) Draw all the lines of symmetry.
(c) Write the total number of lines of symmetry on each shape.
(d) Cut out the shapes and stick them in your exercise book.

2 Name the shapes which have
(a) only one line of symmetry (b) no lines of symmetry
(c) more than one line of symmetry.

3 (a) Use the Shapes sheet.
Repeat questions **1 (b)**, **(c)** and **(d)** for each shape.
(b) Copy and complete a table like this:

| Shape | Number of equal sides | Number of equal angles | Number of lines of symmetry |
|---|---|---|---|
| Equilateral triangle | 3 | 3 | |
| | | | |

What do you notice?

Quasim makes tiled floor designs.

**1** **(a)** Copy each floor design on squared paper.

**(b)** Colour the designs so that each has two lines of symmetry.

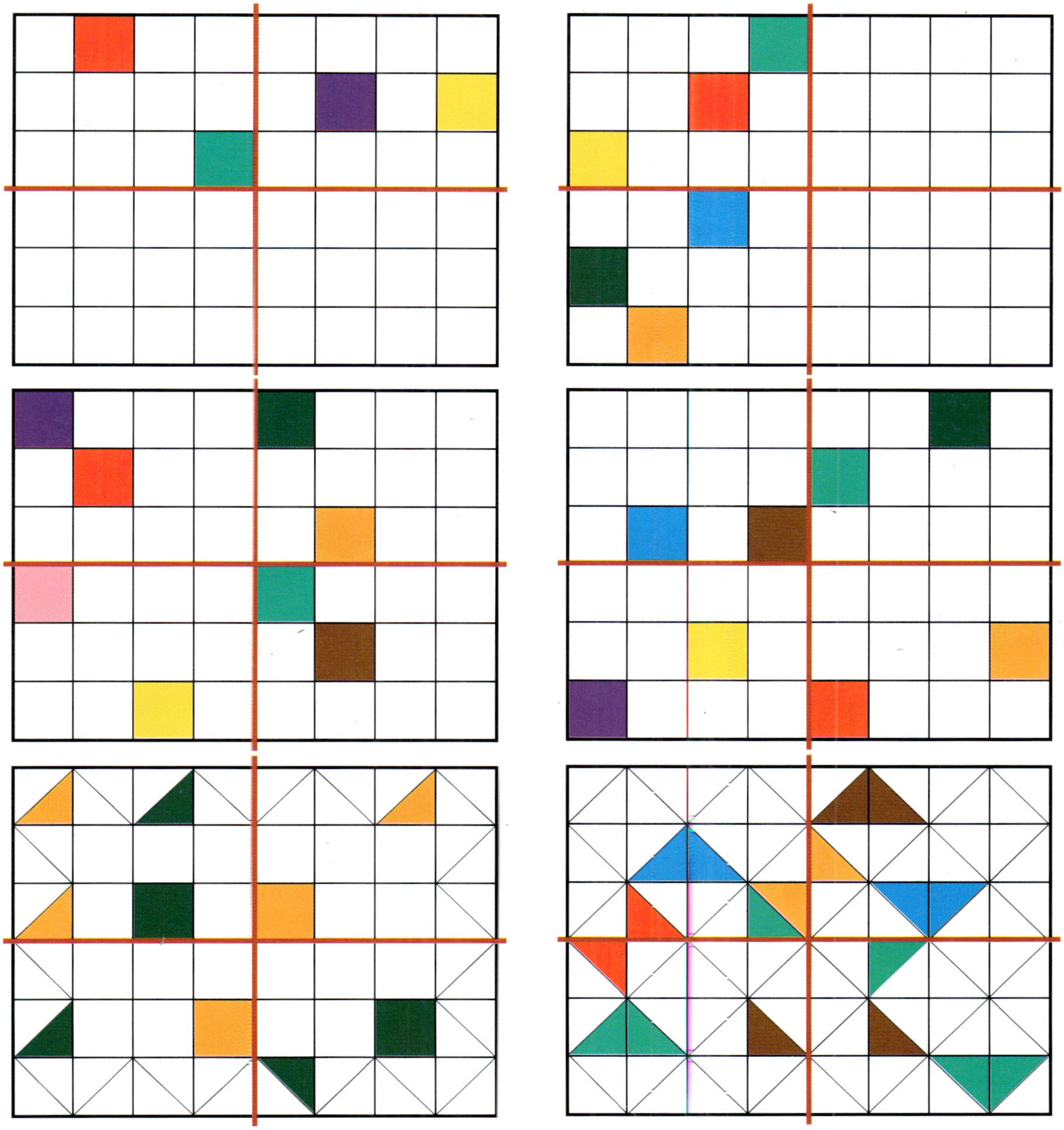

**2** Draw and colour your own floor design.

**You need 3D shapes like these.**

**1** Write the name of each shape. Choose from the labels.

(a) 

(b) 

(c) 

(d) 

(e) 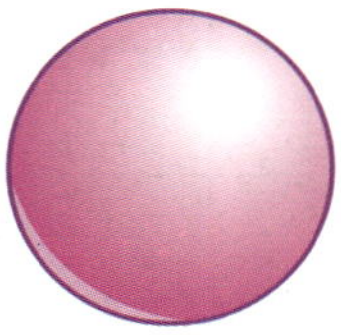

(f) 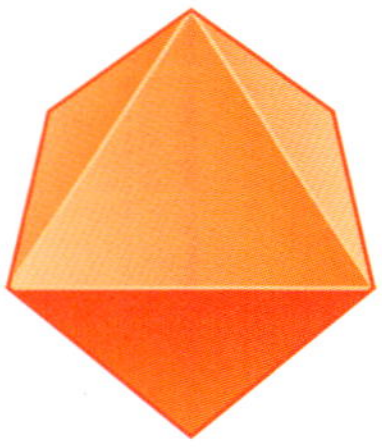

(g) 

(h) 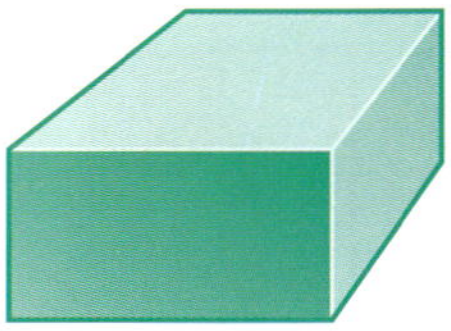

| | | | | |
|---|---|---|---|---|
| triangular prism | cylinder | cube | sphere | pentagonal prism |
| cone | octahedron | hexagonal prism | triangular pyramid | cuboid |

**2** Which shape could be in the bag? Name **two** shapes each time.

(a) 

(b) 

(c) 

(d) 

**3** Write a clue to describe each of these shapes.

(a) 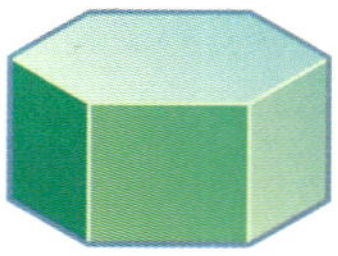

(b) 

(c) 

**1** **(a)** For each net, name the 3D shape.

**(b)** Make each net then construct the shape to check.

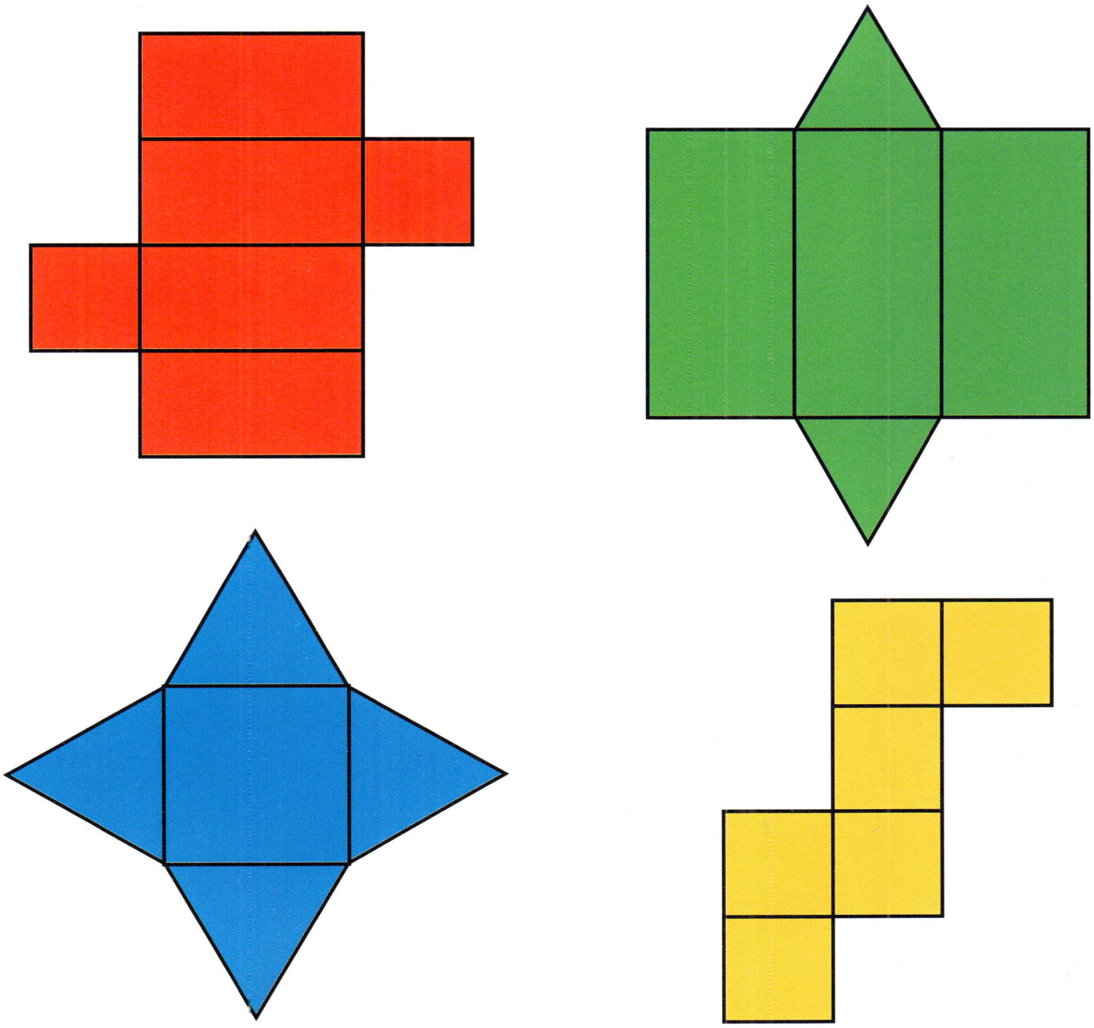

**2** **(a)** Which nets do you **think** will make a box with no lid?

**(b)** Check by joining squares.

1 List the co-ordinates of
- the vertices of each half shape
- the vertices needed to complete each shape so that the **red** line is an axis of symmetry.

**(a)**

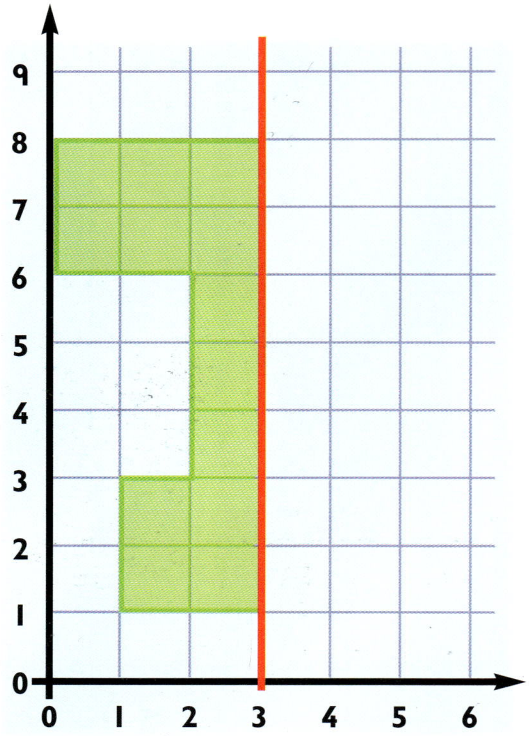

**(b)**

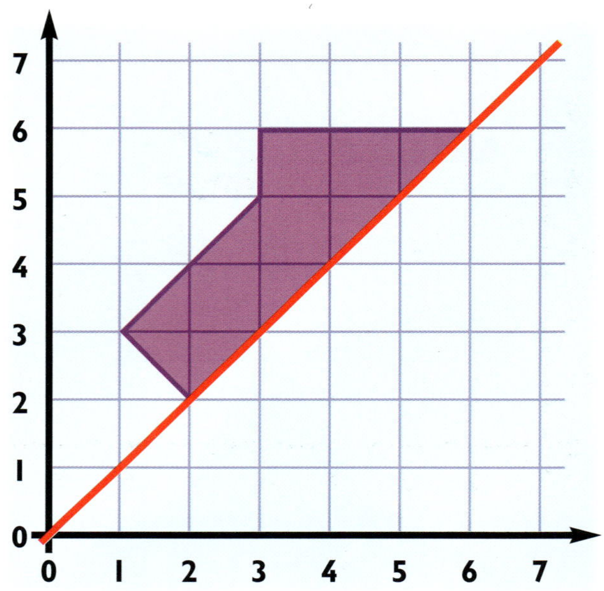

**(c)**

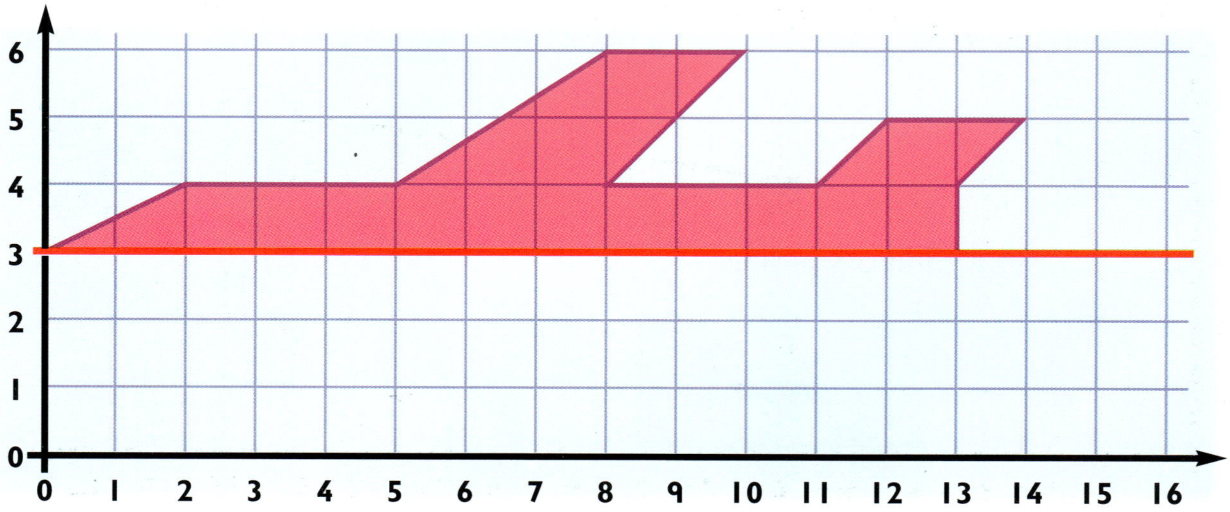

**1** Write the co-ordinates of the **vertex** needed to complete each shape.

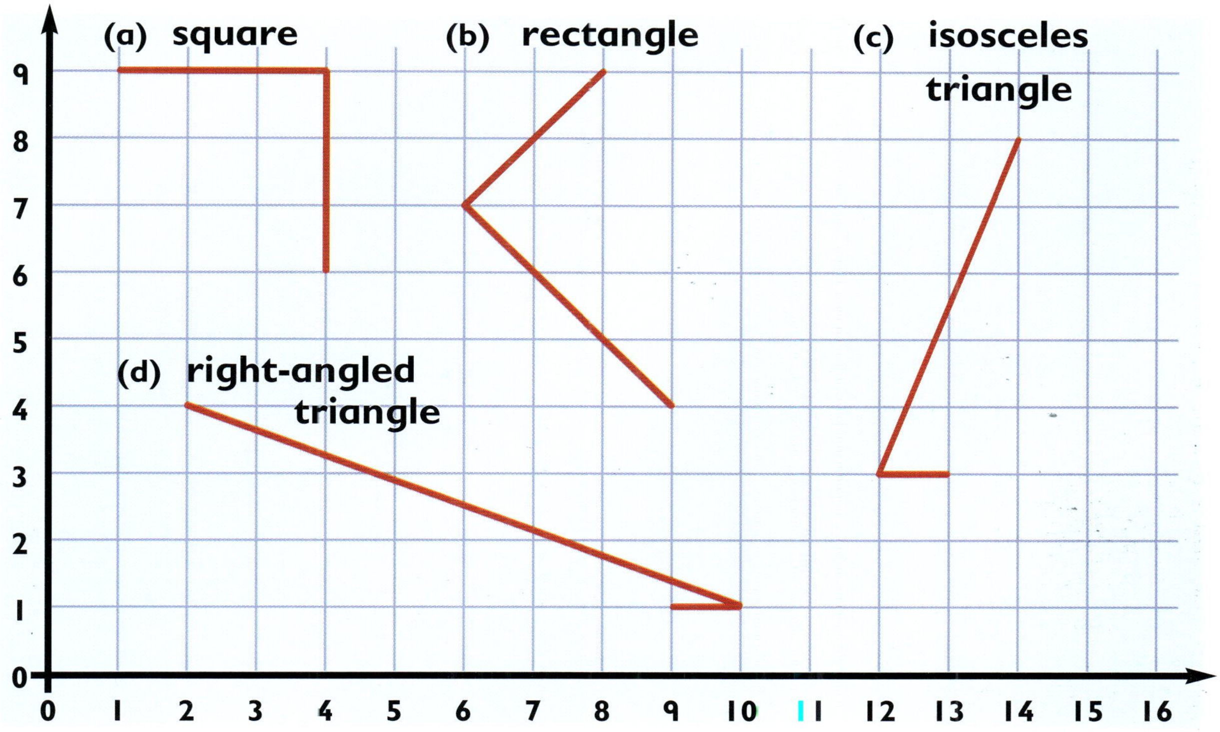


**2** Write the co-ordinates of the **end points** of a line of equal length **and** parallel to

**(a)** the red line **(b)** the black line **(c)** the green line.

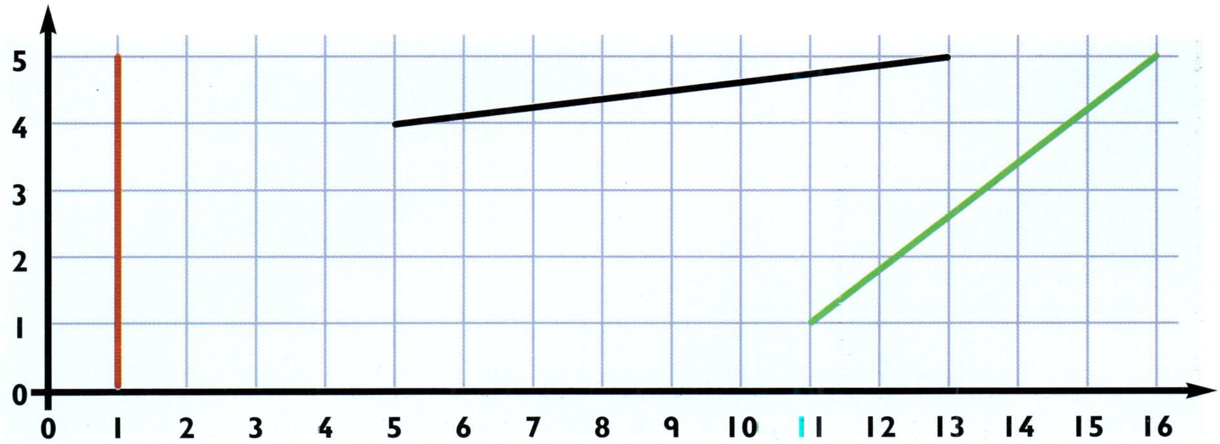

**1** **(a)** Copy the shape on squared paper.
**(b)** Sketch the shape to show its position after it has moved **2 units to the right.**

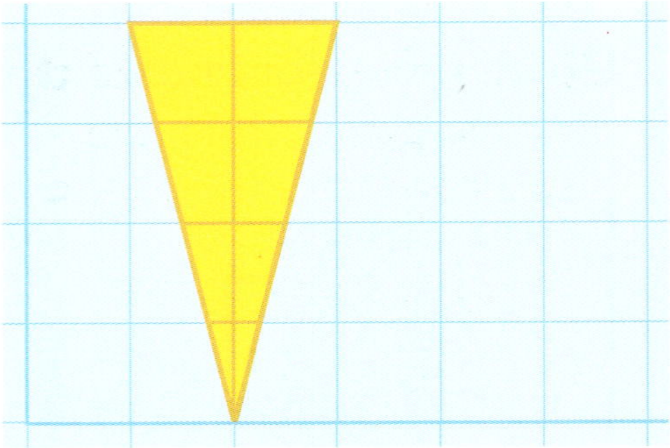

**2** Repeat question **1** for these shapes and movements.

**(a)** **2 units to the left**

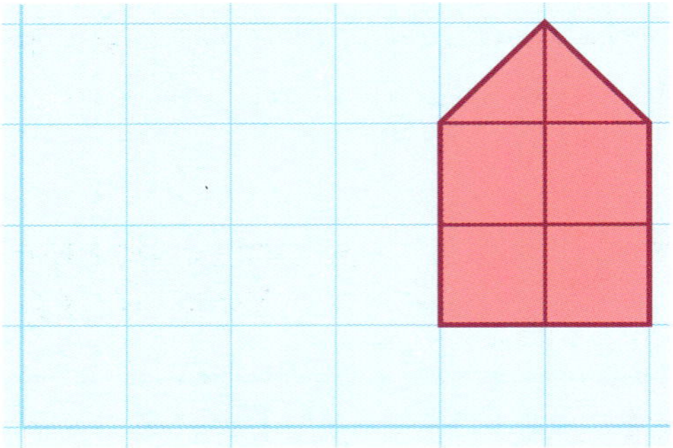

**(b)** **3 units to the right**

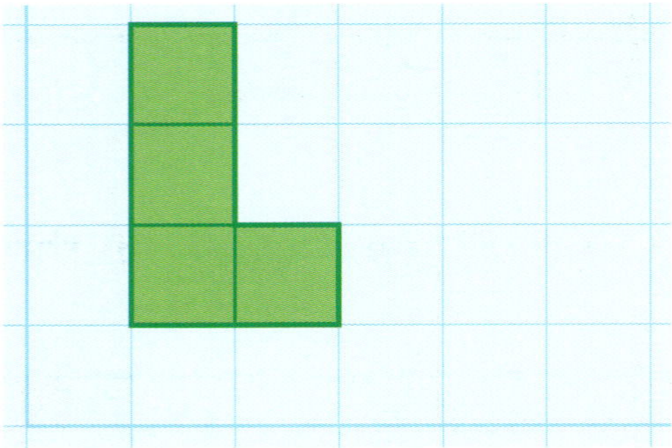

**(c)** **4 units to the right**

**(d)** **3 units to the left**

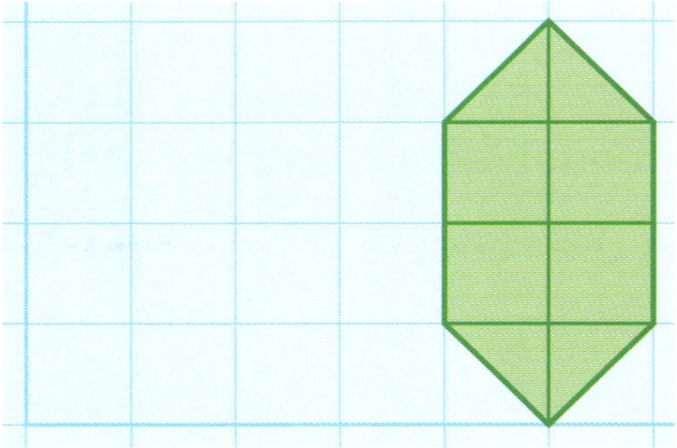

**3** Translate the shape **4 units to the right**. Repeat until the strip is filled.

**1** List the co-ordinates of the vertices of each shape
- in the position shown
- after the shape has moved

**(a)** two units right

**(b)** three units left

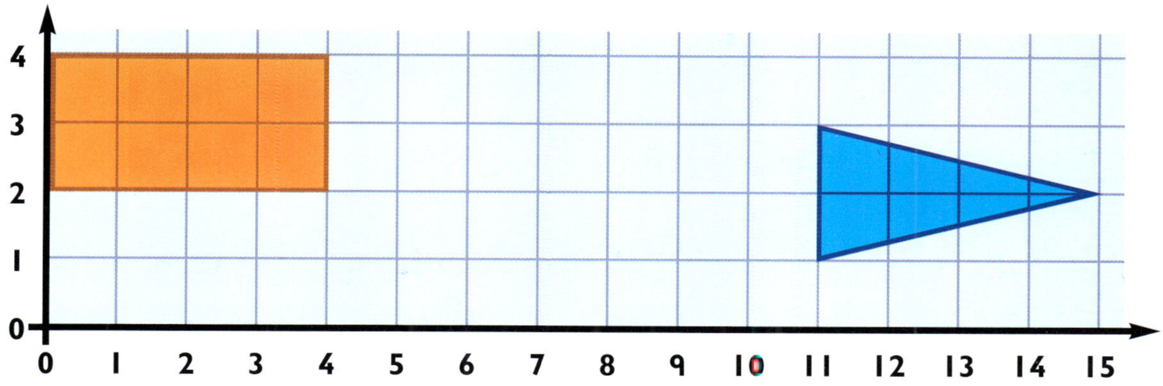

**(c)** one unit up

**(d)** three units down

**(e)** one unit right **and** two units up

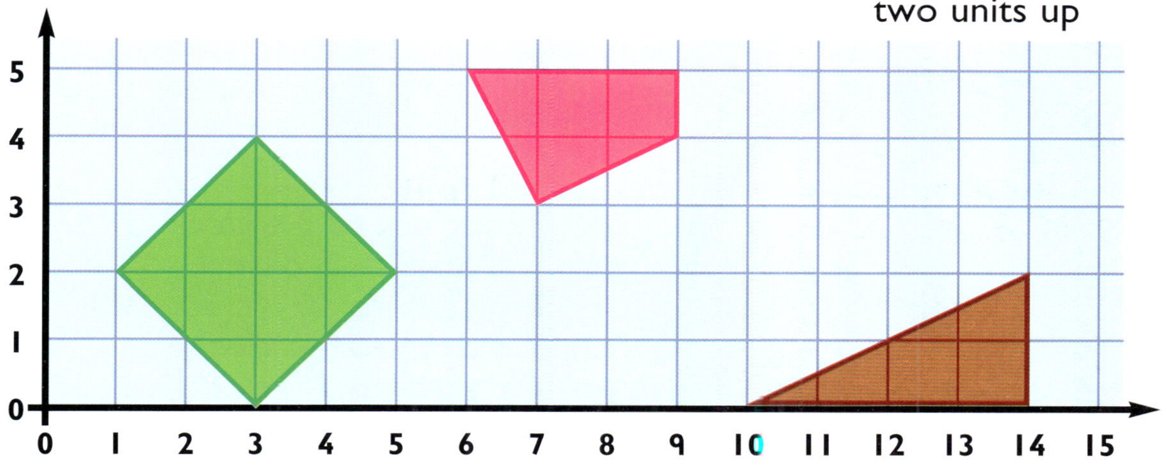

**(f)** six units left **and** two units down.

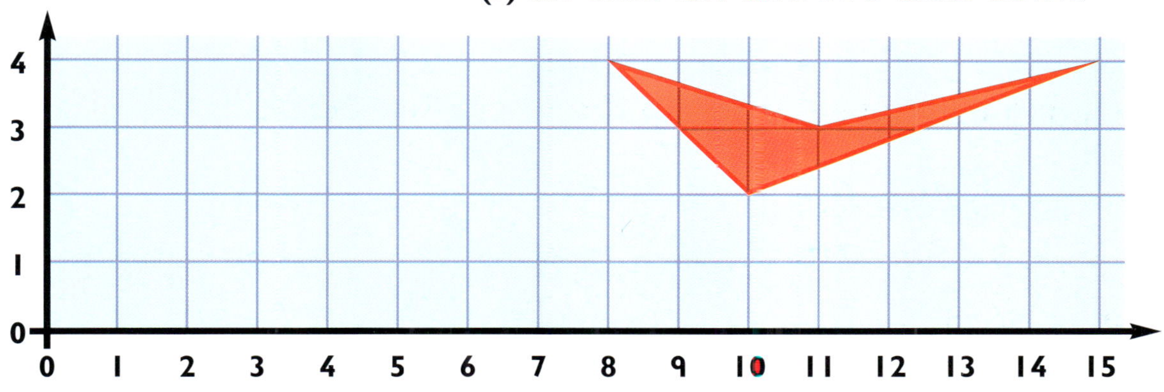

**1** Through how many degrees does the pointer turn when it moves

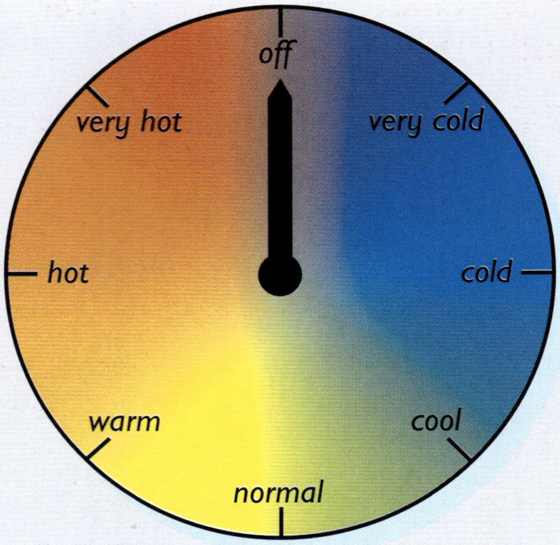


(a) clockwise from *off* to *cold*
(b) anti-clockwise from *hot* to *warm*
(c) clockwise from *very hot* to *cool*
(d) clockwise from *cold* to *warm*
(e) anti-clockwise from *very cold* to *very hot*
(f) clockwise from *warm* to *cool*?

**2** Which setting is the pointer facing after it turns

(a) 45° clockwise from *normal*
(b) 135° anti-clockwise from *off*
(c) 360° anti-clockwise from *hot*
(d) 270° clockwise from *cold*?

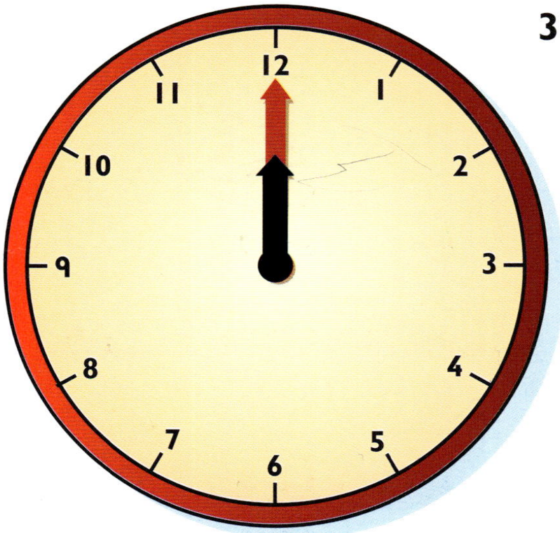


**3** Through how many degrees **clockwise** does the **hour** hand turn when it moves from

(a) 12 o'clock to 3 o'clock
(b) 4 o'clock to 5 o'clock
(c) 8 o'clock to 10 o'clock
(d) 7 o'clock to 1 o'clock
(e) 6 o'clock to 3 o'clock
(f) 5 o'clock to 9 o'clock
(g) 9 o'clock to 2 o'clock
(h) 1 o'clock to 11 o'clock?

**4** What time does the clock show when the hour hand moves clockwise

(a) 60° from 5 o'clock
(b) 180° from 10 o'clock
(c) 270° from 12 o'clock
(d) 330° from 11 o'clock?

The numeral **4** can be written using the commands:

**FD 2 BK 1 RT 90 FD 1**

**BK 2 LT 90 FD 3**

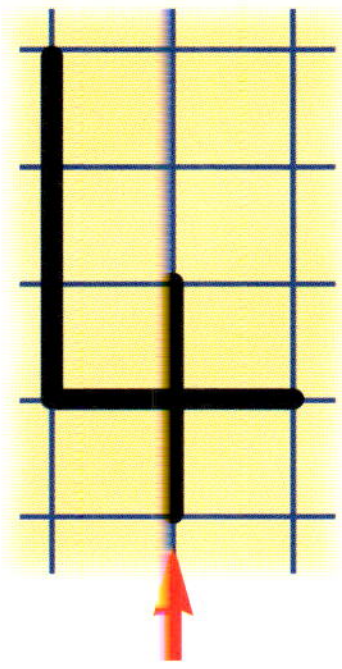

1 Write commands for each of these numerals.
Start with the position and direction shown each time.

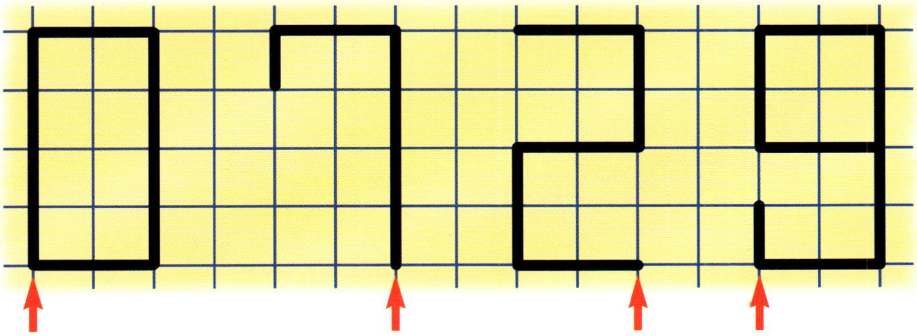

**Use squared paper.**

2 Follow these commands to write other numerals.
Start facing this way ↑ each time.

**(a)** RT 90 FD 2 LT 90 FD 2 LT 90 FD 2
BK 2 RT 90 FD 2 LT 90 FD 2

**(b)** RT 90 FD 2 LT 90 FD 2 LT 90 FD 2
RT 90 FD 2 RT 90 FD 2

**(c)** FD 2 BK 2 RT 90 FD 2 LT 90 FD 2
LT 90 FD 2 RT 90 FD 2 RT 90 FD 2
RT 90 FD 1

3 Write commands to draw the numeral **8**.
Do **not**
- use the command **BK**
- go over the same line more than once.

Draw an arrow to show where you started.

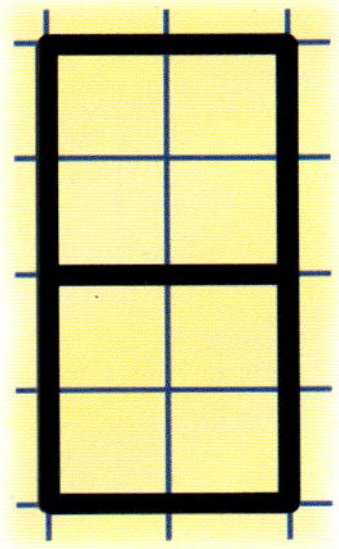

**1** **(a)** Which angles are
• right • acute • obtuse?

**(b)** List the angles in order, starting with the smallest.

**2** Which shape has

**(a)** only two acute and only two obtuse angles
**(b)** two right angles, one acute angle and one obtuse angle
**(c)** **all** of its angles obtuse
**(d)** **none** of its angles obtuse
**(e)** only two acute angles and only one obtuse angle
**(f)** three obtuse angles and one acute angle
**(g)** one right angle, two acute angles and one obtuse angle?

**3** Draw a **quadrilateral** which has two **opposite** acute angles and two **opposite** obtuse angles.

**1** **(a)** **Estimate** the size of each angle **to the nearest 5°.**

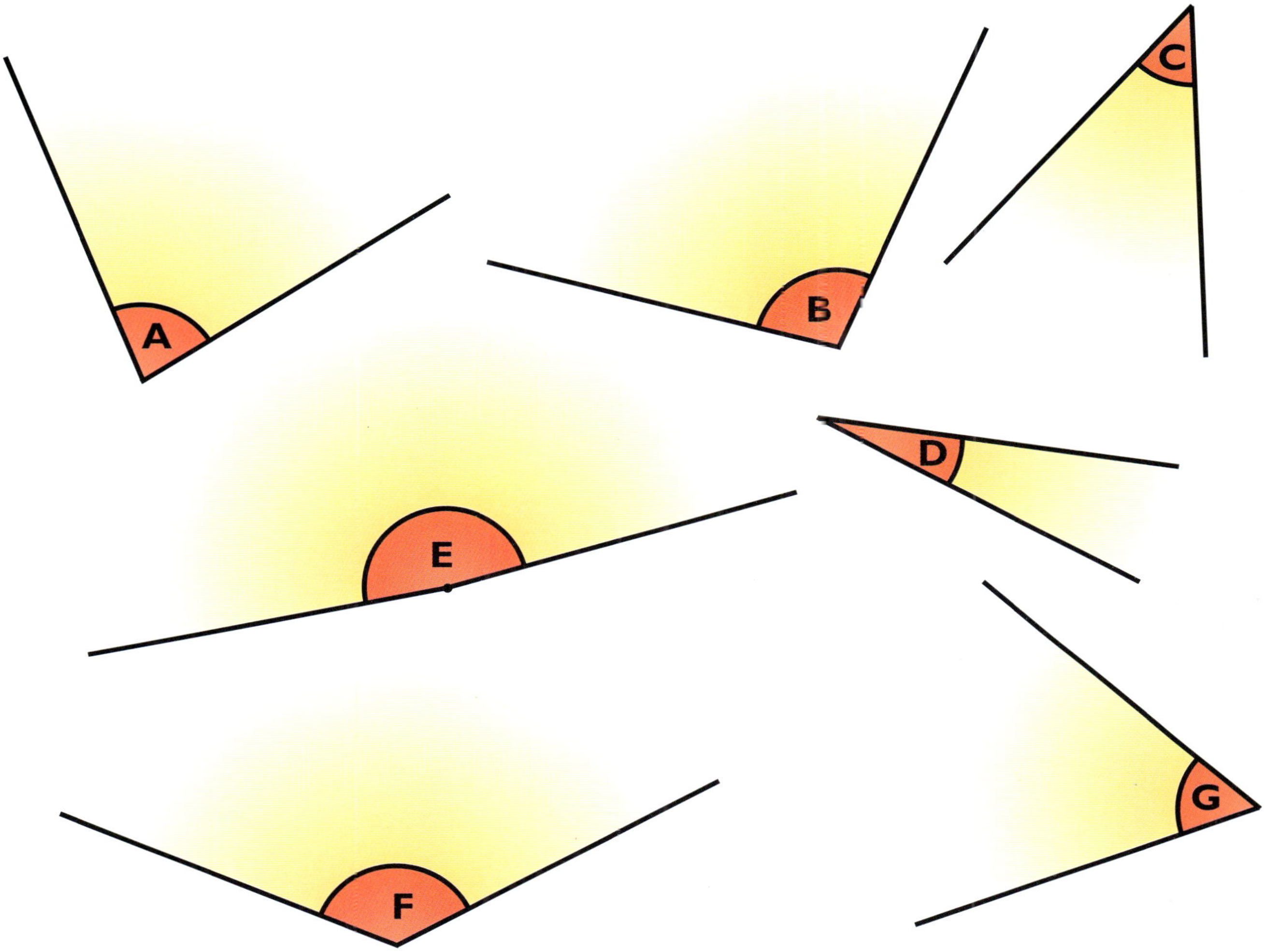


**(b)** Check by **measuring** with a protractor.

**2** **Calculate** the size of each **blue** angle.

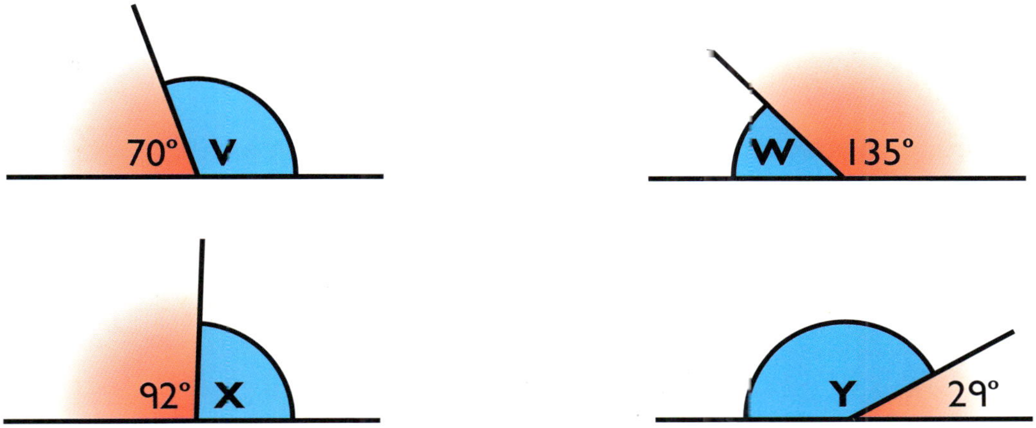

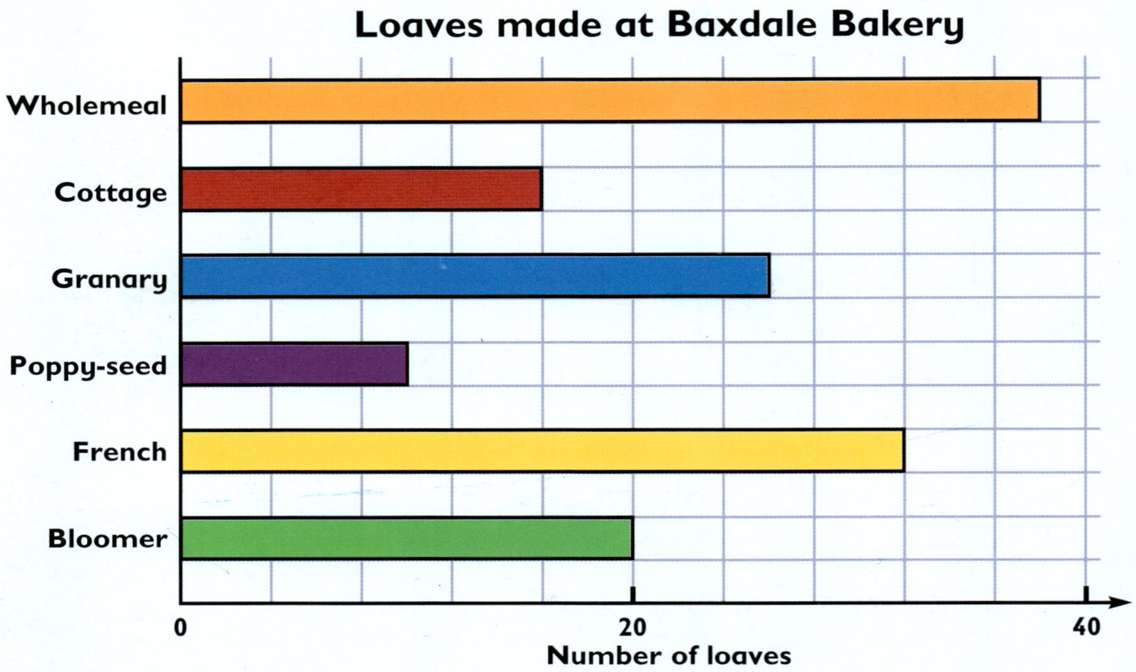


1 Which kind of loaf did the bakery make
(a) most of (b) least of?

2 How many of each kind of loaf were made?

3 How many **fewer** Cottage loaves were made than
(a) French (b) Granary (c) Wholemeal?

4 The bakery made scones for Baxdale School Fayre. Draw a **bar chart** to show the information in the table.

**Scones baked**

| Plain | Fruit | Cherry | Treacle | Bran | Cheese |
|---|---|---|---|---|---|
| 20 | 34 | 14 | 30 | 8 | 28 |

**Drinks bought at Baxdale School Fayre**

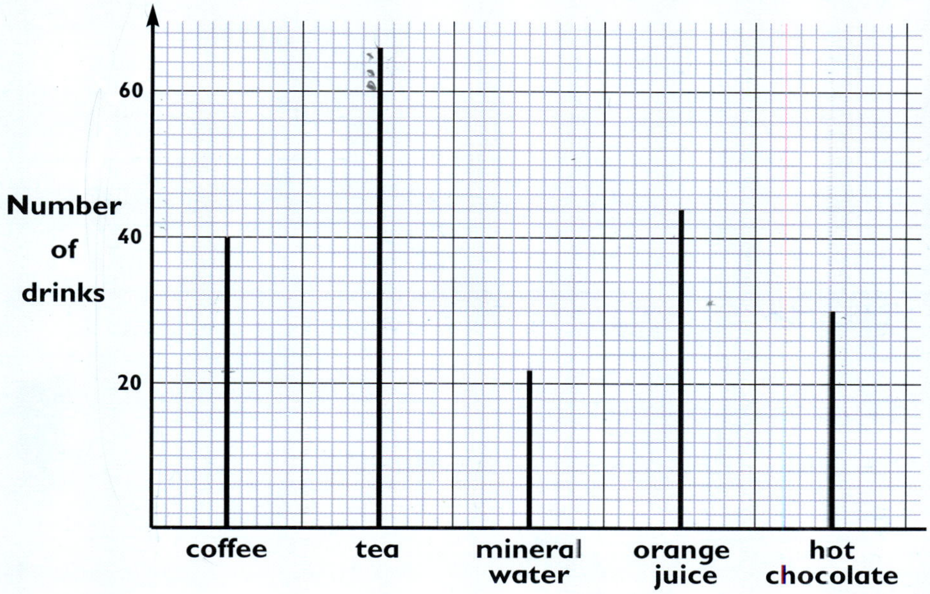

**1** Which drink was the most popular?

**2** How many of each type of drink were bought?

**3** How many drinks were bought altogether?

**4** **(a)** Which drink was twice as popular as mineral water?
**(b)** Suggest a reason for this.

**5** Draw a **bar line chart** to show the information in the table.

**Number of visitors in the café at**

| 10.15 | 10.30 | 10.45 | 11.00 | 11.15 | 11.30 |
|---|---|---|---|---|---|
| 20 | 62 | 54 | 46 | 28 | 12 |

**1** The table has information about special breads from Baxdale Bakery.

| Number of loaves baked | | Colour | Shape | Flour | Finish |
|---|---|---|---|---|---|
| Adrian | 12 | white | round | plain | seeds |
| Lisa | 18 | white | twisted | plain | nuts |
| Bindu | 16 | brown | round | wholemeal | seeds and nuts |
| Pamela | 24 | white | stick | plain | seeds and nuts |
| Jo | 10 | brown | twisted | granary | nuts |
| Scott | 20 | white | round | plain | seeds |

**(a)** How many loaves were baked altogether?

**(b)** Who is correct and who is wrong? Explain.

**2** In which ways are Adrian's and Bindu's loaves

**(a)** the same **(b)** different?

**3** Name each baker.

**(a)**

**(b)**

**(c)**

**(d)**

Class 5 carries out a survey to find out if what their teacher says is true.

**Baxdale School - Letters in boys' names**

| | | |
|---|---|---|
| 3 | 卌 III | |
| 4 | 卌 卌 卌 卌 | |
| 5 | 卌 卌 卌 卌 卌 卌 II | |
| 6 | 卌 卌 卌 卌 卌 卌 | |
| 7 | 卌 卌 | |

**1** (a) How many boys' names have

- 3 letters
- 4 letters
- 5 letters
- 6 letters
- 7 letters?

**Survey of boys' first names**

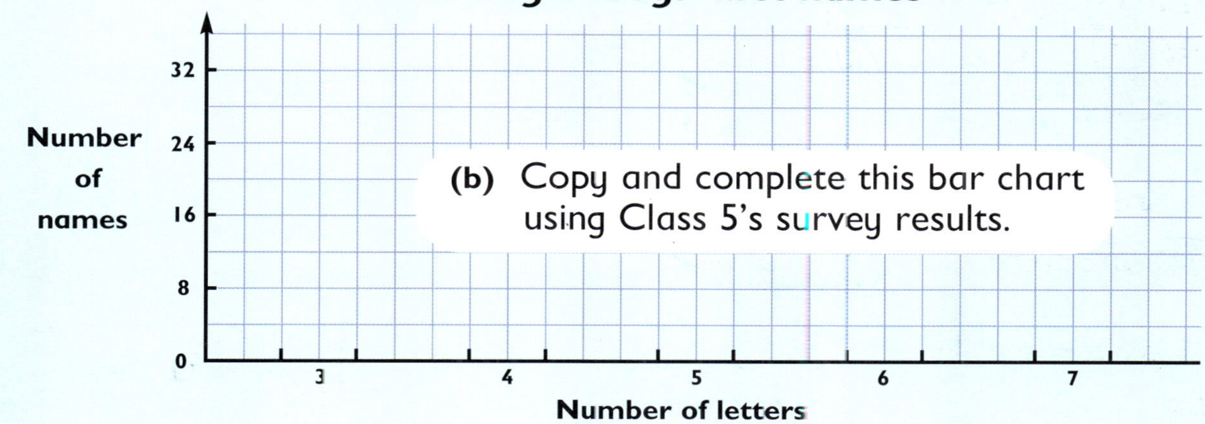


(b) Copy and complete this bar chart using Class 5's survey results.

**2** (a) How many boys' names altogether are in the survey?
(b) Which number of letters in a name is the **mode**?
(c) What **fraction** of the names have 6 letters?

**3** (a) Write the greatest and the smallest number of letters in a name.
(b) What is the **range**?

**4** Is it true that about half of the boys' names have 4 **or** 5 letters? Explain.

The children in your class will be helping in the café.

What chance does each event have of happening at Baxdale School Fayre?

Write **no chance** or **poor chance** or **even chance** or **good chance** or **certain**.

**A** You will go to the Fayre by helicopter.

**B** You will see a classmate.

**C** Something will be spilled.

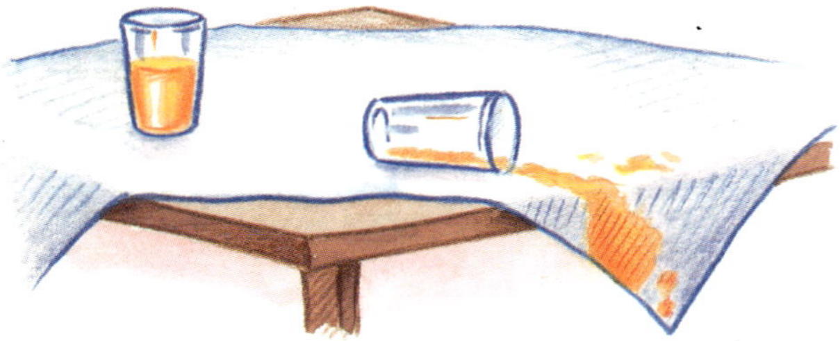

**D** All of the scones will be sold.

**E** No biscuits will be sold.

**F** It will rain.